Activating
GOD'S
Covenant
PROMISES

DR. FESTUS ADEYEYE

ACTIVATING GOD'S COVENANT PROMISES

Published By Cornerstone Publishing

info@thecornerstonepublishers.com
www.thecornerstonepublishers.com

Contact Information

To order bulk copies of this book, please write to:
Dr. Festus Adeyeye
Adeyeye Evangelistic Ministries (AEM)
P.O. Box 810, West Hempstead, NY 11552
drfestus@alcministries.com

CONTENTS

INTRODUCTION

Welcome to your season of covenant fulfillment. This is not just another book—it is a divine invitation to step into the manifestation of God's promises for your life. The Scriptures declare in Joshua 21:43-45: *"So the Lord gave to Israel all the land of which He had sworn to give to their fathers, and they took possession of it and dwelt in it. The Lord gave them rest all around, according to all that He had sworn to their fathers. And not a man of all their enemies stood against them; the Lord delivered all their enemies into their hands. Not a word failed of any good thing which the Lord had spoken to the house of Israel. All came to pass."*

This passage is a profound reminder that God is not only a promise-giver but also a promise-keeper. He does not offer empty words or make fleeting declarations. Every promise He has spoken carries the weight of divine certainty, and He watches over His Word to perform it. Yet, many believers struggle to see these promises manifest in their lives. Why? Because while God's promises are sure, they require activation. Just as Israel had to rise and take possession of the land, we must take spiritual steps to unlock the fulfillment of God's covenant promises in our lives.

In a world of broken promises, where trust is often betrayed and expectations are dashed, God stands apart. He is faithful, unchanging, and true to His Word. He does not guess at what

He will do—He declares it and brings it to pass. When God visited Sarah, He fulfilled the word He had spoken: *"And the Lord visited Sarah as He had said, and the Lord did unto Sarah as He had spoken. For Sarah conceived and bore Abraham a son in his old age, at the set time of which God had spoken to him."* (Genesis 21:1-2)

This is the pattern of God—He speaks, and then He acts. His Word is the catalyst for His works. Where His promises are declared, divine visitation and manifestation follow. This truth is as relevant today as it was in biblical times. God still visits, God still speaks, and God still fulfills.

Why must God's promises come to pass? Because they are not ordinary words; they are covenant words. The Bible contains thousands of promises—each one backed by divine assurance. Scripture affirms: *"My covenant I will not break, nor alter the word that has gone out of My lips."* (Psalm 89:34)

A covenant is an irrevocable agreement, sealed by God's own oath. Hebrews 6:13-18 reminds us that God swore by Himself because there was no greater authority. His promises are not subject to human limitations. The passage of time cannot weaken them, and opposition cannot overturn them. *"Heaven and earth will pass away, but My words will by no means pass away."* (Luke 21:33)

What has God spoken concerning your life, your family, your health, and your destiny? No matter how long it has seemed delayed, be assured that God's Word will come to pass. If He did it for Israel, He will do it for you.

God's promises are already fulfilled in Christ, but it is our responsibility to lay hold of them. This book is your guide to unlocking divine fulfillment. Through faith, prayer, obedience, and a deeper understanding of God's covenant nature, you will learn how to stand on His Word with unwavering confidence, overcome delay and opposition, align your life with covenant principles, and take possession of what God has already declared yours.

The time for waiting and wondering is over. It is time to step into your divine inheritance. Just as the Israelites took possession of the Promised Land, you are about to walk into the fullness of all that God has ordained for you. This is your moment. This is your season. Get ready—God's covenant promises are about to manifest in your life!

PART 1

FOUNDATIONAL TRUTHS ABOUT GOD'S COVENANT PROMISES

CHAPTER 1

THE PROMISE-KEEPING GOD

"God is not a man, that He should lie…"

(Numbers 23:19)

One of the hardest things in today's world is knowing whose words to believe or trust. Many of us have been victims of unreliable people who disappointed us with unfulfilled promises. However, in a world of broken promises, God can be counted on. He is always faithful and remains committed to fulfilling His promises. His words do not fail; they are reliable and dependable.

God does not play around with His Word. He has a plan for everyone, and the fulfillment of His promises is the actualization of His plan for our lives. When He speaks, His words accomplish His purposes. His counsel stands forever, and He doesn't just give promises - He keeps them. You can be sure that God's promises will be fulfilled in your life.

God's declarations are eternal, unchanging, and backed by divine power. From the rising of the sun to the breath in our lungs, every moment of existence testifies to His faithfulness. When we place our hope in God, we anchor ourselves in a truth that never wavers.

Throughout history, countless lives have been transformed by the knowledge that God is faithful. His promises are not mere hopeful wishes but divine commitments, designed to bring about transformation in every season of life. Trusting in Him gives you the courage to face adversity. His Word is a firm foundation that can be trusted.

ATTRIBUTES OF GOD'S PROMISE-KEEPING NATURE

God's ability to keep His promises is rooted in His very nature. Unlike human beings, whose limitations often prevent them from fulfilling their commitments, God operates beyond time, resources, and changing circumstances. His faithfulness is not based on emotions or external factors—it is an unchanging attribute of His divine character.

Several key aspects of God's nature guarantee that His promises will never fail.

1. Perfect Faithfulness

At the very core of God's nature lies His perfect faithfulness. Unlike humans, who may break promises due to changing circumstances, limited abilities, or shifting loyalties, God's promise-keeping flows from His immutable character. His faithfulness isn't just what He does—it's who He is. He declares in Malachi 3:6, *"For I am the Lord, I change not."*

This unchanging nature ensures that when God makes a promise, it's already settled in heaven. Time itself bends to His will, and circumstances align to fulfill His word.

2. Infinite Power To Fulfill

Human promises often fail because of limited resources or ability. We might promise with sincere hearts but lack the power to deliver. God, however, possesses infinite power to fulfill every promise He makes. The creation of the universe itself stands as a testament to His ability—He spoke, and worlds formed.

This unlimited power means that no promise is too big for God to keep. Whether it's parting seas, raising the dead, or transforming hearts of stone into hearts of flesh, His ability matches His commitment.

THE CONTRAST BETWEEN GOD'S PROMISES AND HUMAN PROMISES

Even when made with the best intentions, human promises carry inherent limitations, some of which are:

- **Limited knowledge of the future**: Humans can only make educated guesses about tomorrow. Our best predictions and plans are based on patterns and probabilities, which unforeseen circumstances can easily derail. We make promises based on our current understanding, which may later prove inadequate. Economic changes, natural disasters, or personal crises can invalidate our commitments. Our inability to see the full implications of our promises often leads to unintended complications

- **Finite resources and abilities**: We often overestimate our capabilities when making commitments, yet humans are limited in many ways. Physical limitations restrict what we can accomplish. Financial constraints affect our ability to fulfill monetary promises. Time is a finite resource we cannot multiply, and fluctuations in energy and health impact our capacity to deliver. Even our skills and talents have natural boundaries, and access to necessary resources may change unexpectedly.

- **Susceptibility to changing circumstances**: Nothing on earth is permanent; change is the only constant thing here. Job losses can prevent financial commitments from being honored. Relationships change, affecting interpersonal promises. Unexpected health issues may arise. External factors beyond our control can force promise-breaking. Emotional states fluctuate, affecting our commitment levels. Social and political changes can force us to break our promises. Family emergencies may force us to prioritize differently. All these factors and more make humans susceptible to failure in fulfilling their promises.

- **Imperfect understanding of consequences:** Humans rarely grasp the full impact of their promises at the moment they make them. What seems reasonable in one season may become impossible in another. In the heat of emotion, a man might promise his beloved the world - but is the world really his to give to anyone?

- **Mortality and time constraints**: Even if a person has the full capacity to fulfill a promise, death can cut life short. Shifting priorities across different life stages can alter commitment levels, and even memory issues can affect promise-keeping.

These human limitations often lead to broken promises - not necessarily from malice, but from human frailty. Humans simply cannot guarantee outcomes the way God can. With God, there is no limitation or constraint. He can fully deliver on every promise. In fact, the Bible declares that He is able to do exceedingly abundantly, above all we can ever ask or think (Ephesians 3:20)!

Isn't that mind-blowing? Do you realize the weight of those words? It means if you ask God for ten and He promises to give you, He is fully capable of giving you a million instead!

DIVINE PERFECTION

God's promises transcend all limitations.

- **He exists outside of time**: God is not limited by time; He created time, so He cannot be controlled by it. The One who was, who is, and who is to come sees the past, present, and future simultaneously. His promises are made with perfect knowledge of all timeframes. Time constraints do not limit His ability to fulfill His promises. He can orchestrate events across centuries. His timing is perfect because He sees the complete picture. Promises made in eternity past remain valid in the present, and future fulfillment is as certain as past accomplishment.

- **He possesses perfect knowledge of all possibilities**: Our God is omniscient. He knows every potential outcome of every situation, so nothing takes Him by surprise. He sees all consequences, both immediate and eternal. His knowledge encompasses every detail of creation. All variables and possible scenarios are accounted for in His promises. Nothing occurs outside God's awareness or permission, so He is perfectly able to do everything He promises.

- **His resources are infinite**: All resources belong to God. Silver and gold are His; so, no promise is too costly for Him to fulfill. He can create *ex nihilo* (out of nothing). Just as He did when He fed thousands with five loaves of bread and two fishes, He can multiply resources as needed. His abundance never runs dry.

- **His power knows no bounds**: God is omnipotent; He can do all things. Nothing is too difficult for Him. Natural laws submit to His authority. Distance is no obstacle to Him. His promises are backed by His omnipotence.

- **His character never changes**: God's nature is immutable. His faithfulness is constant, His love is unshakeable, and His mercy endures forever. He will fulfill His promises to you.

BIBLICAL FOUNDATIONS OF GOD'S FAITHFULNESS

The Bible is filled with assurances of God's fidelity. Below are some examples:

> *"For as the rain cometh down, and the snow from heaven, and returneth not thither, but watereth the earth, and maketh it bring forth and bud, that it may give seed to the sower, and bread to the eater: So shall my word be that goeth forth out of my mouth: it shall not return unto me void, but it shall accomplish that which I please, and it shall prosper in the thing whereto I sent it"* (Isaiah 55:10-11, KJV).

In the passage above, God's Word is compared to the nourishing rain and snow that bring forth abundant harvests. Think about this – have you ever seen rain fall while the ground remains dry? Many human activities, especially agriculture, depend on rainfall and the changing seasons, and God's purpose in them is always fulfilled. Just as rainfall ensures an abundant harvest, God's promises guarantee fulfillment. Every utterance from God's mouth will achieve its purpose.

> *"For You have magnified Your word above all Your name"* (Psalm 138:2).

This scripture declares that God's Word is exalted above even His own name—an indication of its supreme authority.

God's name is powerful, but His Word is even greater. Some people place little or no value on their words, but God honors and magnifies His Word above His name. This gives us absolute assurance that His Word will be magnified in our lives.

> *"So the LORD gave to Israel all the land of which He had sworn to give to their fathers, and they took possession of it and dwelt in it. The LORD gave them rest all around, according to all that He had sworn to their fathers. And not a man of all their enemies stood against them; the LORD delivered all their enemies into their hand. Not a word failed of any good thing which the LORD had spoken to the house of Israel. All came to pass"* (Joshua 21:43-45).

In this present year and throughout the years of your life, not a word will fail of any good thing that God has spoken to you.

> *"In hope of eternal life, which God, that cannot lie, promised before the world began"* (Titus 1:2, KJV).

It is not that God chooses not to lie; He cannot lie. He has no ability to lie.

These scriptures, among many others, illustrate a fundamental truth: God's promises are irrevocable. His covenant with His people is sealed by an eternal oath (Hebrews 6:17). This unchanging nature of God's Word gives believers confidence in facing trials, knowing that every promise He makes is destined to be fulfilled.

GOD'S PROMISES ARE BACKED BY HIS POWER

The counsel, plan, and mandate of God for your life are backed by His ability to fulfill them. Sometimes, people want to help you but lack the ability to do so. However, God's promises are never limited by human weaknesses—they are backed by His divine abilities.

The question is, is there anything too hard for God? The One who created the universe, does He not have the power to fulfill what He has promised? His capacity is unlimited, and His ability is boundless. The heavens and the earth may pass away, but His words will never fail (Matthew 24:35).

God is not human that He should lie. If He has given you His word, He will fulfill it.

Consider this:

When an American ambassador is sent to another country, his personal status does not determine his authority. He is respected not because of his stature, but because of the power and resources of the nation he represents. If you touch an American ambassador, you have touched the entire United States—its people, its military, its government.

In the same way, God's Word is backed by His limitless power and sovereignty. This sovereign power can override situations and seasons. Neither human permutations nor satanic manipulations can affect God; nothing can stop the manifestation of His supreme purpose.

No matter the agenda of the enemy, what God has promised will come to fulfilment. Nothing can overcome God; therefore, understand that no matter what you are passing through or what may befall you, you will overcome with God on your side.

All of God's promises are already fulfilled in Christ. So, when you claim them, don't see them as mere words from man. Jesus completed them on the cross when He declared, *Tetelestai*— "It is finished; paid in full." Through His obedience on the cross, He secured every promise of God for us. The only way to nullify God's promises would be to undo what Christ has accomplished—and that is impossible. It's a done deal— fulfilled and waiting to manifest in your life!

"For all the promises of God in him are yea, and in him Amen, unto the glory of God by us" (2 Corinthians 1:20, KJV).

WHY DIVINE PROMISES MATTER

Believing in a promise-keeping God transforms our perspective on life. Divine promises are the blueprint for our future—they guide our decisions, bolster our faith in trials, and illuminate the path toward spiritual growth. When we align our lives with these promises, we step into a realm where hope is not an abstract concept but a living reality.

For many, trusting in God's promises means understanding that every difficulty has a purpose and every delay is an opportunity for deeper transformation. As we continue through the pages of this book, may you come to see that the promises of God are the very heartbeat of a victorious life.

Now that we have established who God is—a faithful and unchanging Promise Keeper—let us explore the very nature of the fulfillment of His promises.

CHAPTER 2

THE FULFILLMENT OF DIVINE PROMISES

"And the Lord visited Sarah as he had said, and the Lord did unto Sarah as he had spoken. For Sarah conceived, and bare Abraham a son in his old age, at the set time of which God had spoken to him. And Abraham called the name of his son that was born unto him, whom Sarah bare to him, Isaac"

(Genesis 21:1–3, KJV).

Pay careful attention to the words - *"the Lord visited Sarah as he had said and…did unto Sarah as he had spoken."*

No statement defines fulfillment better.

Fulfillment happens when what God has spoken about you comes to pass. Understand that God never acts outside His Word, and He never speaks without acting on what He has said. The spoken word of God is the catalyst for the acts of

God. God's doings and visitations are always a result of what He has said. God is moved to act upon a life by what He has declared.

The acts of God always follow His words. Covenant promises usually result in divine visitation and divine manifestations. God visited Sarah and brought the fulfillment of covenant promises. If God has promised you, rest assured that He will act for you.

When God fulfills His promises to His people, He also restores time. The fulfillment of God's promises to Sarah also brought the restoration of her lost time. The years she spent waiting for the fruit of the womb were restored.

The season of fulfillment ushers in joy and laughter. The name "Isaac" means "Laughter". In other words, when God's promises to Sarah were fulfilled, there was joy and laughter. The manifestations of God in this season will produce joy, laughter, and gladness—**not just in your life but in the lives of those connected to you.**

What are the covenant promises God has given over your life and family? What has He said concerning you? Get ready for the activation and manifestation. This is the set time for the fulfillment of those long-awaited covenant promises.

IMPLICATIONS OF DIVINE FULFILLMENT

The fulfillment of divine promises is the moment when God's word spoken over an individual, family or situation comes to pass. While the specifics of this may differ for each individual, one thing is certain—divine fulfillment brings joy and gladness.

To better understand what fulfillment of divine promises encompasses, consider it in the following ways:

- **The completion and manifestation of God's plan:** The fulfillment of divine promises is the realization of God's plan for an individual, a family, or an institution. It is the moment when what God has spoken over a person's life comes to pass, confirming His faithfulness. Joshua 21:43-45 testifies to this truth, revealing how the Lord gave Israel all the land He had promised to their ancestors. They took possession of it and settled there, and not a single promise made by the Lord remained unfulfilled. This proves the certainty and reliability of God's word in bringing about His purposes.

- **Experiencing answers to prayers and long-awaited desires:** Fulfillment is when you witness the manifestation of what you have been praying and waiting for. The fulfillment of divine promises turns hope into reality, as seen in the life of Sarah. Genesis 21:1-3 records how the Lord visited Sarah and fulfilled His promise to her, making her to conceive and give birth to Isaac in her old age. Divine fulfillment is often preceded by a period of patient waiting and unwavering faith.

- **A movement from promise to performance:** The fulfillment of God's promises signifies a shift from expectation to realization. It marks the transition from

15

a season of persistent prayer to a season of testimony. This shift is beautifully illustrated in the story of Hannah in 1 Samuel 1:27-28. After years of praying fervently for a child, she finally held Samuel in her arms, testifying that the Lord had answered her prayers. When divine promises are fulfilled, what was once an unseen hope becomes a tangible reality.

- **When sowing becomes reaping and expectations become manifestations:** Fulfillment is the divine turning point where diligent sowing yields a bountiful harvest. It is the season when long-held expectations become concrete manifestations, and whispered prayers turn into loud testimonies. Hannah's journey in 1 Samuel 1 exemplifies this, as she transitioned from barrenness and deep sorrow to joyous celebration with the birth of her son. This is a fulfillment of the scriptural principle that those who sow in tears will reap in joy (Psalm 126:5).

- **The acceleration of divine purposes:** When God fulfills His promises, there is often a supernatural acceleration of His plans. Delays are shattered, and His spoken word is hastened into action. Ezekiel 12:28 says, *"Therefore say unto them, thus saith the Lord God; There shall none of my words be prolonged any more, but the word which I have spoken shall be done, saith the Lord God"* (KJV). This scripture reassures us that divine fulfillment is not subject to human timelines; once God declares that the appointed time has come, nothing can hinder the manifestation of His word.

- **The termination of barrenness and commencement of fruitfulness:** Divine fulfillment causes a shift from a barren season to one of abundant fruitfulness. As Luke 1:57 (TLB) says, *"By now Elizabeth's waiting was over, for the time had come for the baby to be born—and it was a boy."* This scripture captures Elizabeth's long-awaited moment of fulfilment—her waiting ended, and she gave birth to a son. The moment marked the transformation of her life from years of unfulfilled longing to a time of divine joy and testimony. Just as Elizabeth's barrenness was replaced with fruitfulness, divine fulfillment brings an end to prolonged waiting and ushers in a season of tangible blessings.

- **The satisfaction of hope and expectation:** To experience fulfillment is to see one's hopes and expectations come to life. Proverbs 23:18 (KJV) declares, *"For surely there is an end; and thine expectation shall not be cut off."* This verse affirms that no matter how long the wait, God's promises will surely come to pass. Divine fulfillment ensures that faith is not in vain but is rewarded in due time, reinforcing the trustworthiness of God's Word.

- **Moving from the wilderness to the promised land:** Fulfillment signifies a journey completed—a movement from wandering in uncertainty to settling in the land of promise. Just as the Israelites moved from the wilderness into Canaan, so does the fulfillment of God's promises bring believers into their destined place

17

of rest and inheritance. It is a divine assurance that trials and tests are not permanent but will give way to seasons of stability, joy, and peace.

- **The open reward for secret sacrifices:** Divine fulfillment is when hidden burdens, sacrifices, and laborious prayers receive open recognition and reward. God sees the unseen struggles, the silent prayers, and the sacrifices made in secret. At His appointed time, He rewards them openly. Matthew 6:6 assures us of this truth, saying, *"Your Father who sees in secret will reward you openly."* The fulfillment of divine promises is God's way of publicly displaying His faithfulness to those who have steadfastly trusted Him in the private chambers of their faith journey.

WHY YOU MUST BELIEVE THAT GOD'S WORD WILL BE FULFILLED

Circumstances may dictate otherwise but your faith in God's promises must be steadfast. There are more than enough reasons to keep hope alive. Let's see some of them:

1. God Is A Covenant-Keeping God

God packages His promises in a covenant. The Bible is a book of covenant promises from God. There are approximately 3,600 to 8,810 divine promises in the Bible. Each of these is not just a promise but a covenant promise. Understand that a covenant is deeper than a promise; it is an irrevocable agreement, sealed by an oath. God's covenant with us is based on the sacrificial atonement of Jesus Christ. It is an unchangeable, divinely imposed legal agreement between God and man. God has assured in Psalm 89:34, *"My covenant I will not break, Nor alter the word that has gone out of My lips."* So whatever He promises you is not just a word but also a divine certainty. It carries divine insurance and backing. As Hebrews 6:13-18 (KJV) *declares, "For when God made promise to Abraham, because he could swear by no greater, he sware by himself, Saying, Surely blessing I will bless thee, and multiplying I will multiply thee. And so, after he had patiently endured, he obtained the promise. For men verily swear by the greater: and an oath for confirmation is to them an end of all strife. Wherein God, willing more abundantly to shew unto the heirs of promise the immutability of his counsel, confirmed it by an oath: That by two immutable things, in which it was impossible for God to lie, we might have a strong consolation, who have fled for refuge to lay hold upon the hope set before us."*

2. God fulfills His promises because it is a reflection of his nature and character.

God's inherent nature is one of truth and faithfulness, making it impossible for Him to break a promise. He keeps His word because faithfulness is an essential part of His being. He cannot lie.

> *"God is not a man, that He would lie, Nor a son of man, that He would change His mind; Has He said, and will He not do it? Or has He spoken, and will He not make it good?* (Numbers 23:19, NASB).

God's counsel, mandate, and plans for your life are backed by His power to fulfill them. God is the unshakeable force behind

His promises and will bring them to pass! *"Heaven and earth will pass away, but My words will by no means pass away"* (Luke 21:33).

God does not guess what He will do with your life. He has plans for each day and each year of your life. His plans are rooted in His words. God's mandate stands forever.

> *"But the plans of the Lord stand firm forever, the purposes of his heart through all generations"* Psalms 33:11 (NIV).

3. All of God's promises are already fulfilled in Christ.

All the conditions for the fulfillment of divine promises have been met by Christ on our behalf. Therefore, we can change every "if" to "since". Since Christ has fulfilled all the Father's conditions, then all God's promises are guaranteed through Him. Jesus Christ is God's Amen—the divine confirmation of every promise.

> *"For all the promises of God in Him are Yes, and in Him Amen, to the glory of God through us"* (2 Corinthians 1:20).

> *"These are the words of the Amen, the faithful and true witness, the ruler of God's creation"* (Revelation 3:14, NIV).

4. Human impossibility does not affect the fulfillment of God's promises.

Nothing can stop the manifestations of God's promises when He is ready. Time does not affect the certainty of their fulfillment. God's counsel or mandate may be delayed but it cannot be destroyed, no matter the agenda of the enemy. It shall come to pass, irrespective of who or what confronts it.

"So the wall was finished in the twenty and fifth day of the month Elul, in fifty and two days. And it came to pass, that when all our enemies heard thereof, and all the heathen that were about us saw these things, they were much cast down in their own eyes: for they perceived that this work was wrought of our God" (Nehemiah 6:15-16, KJV).

There might be a negative verdict on your life, but God's counsel shall be established. We are in an era where God is still doing the impossible. A couple was once advised to terminate a pregnancy because the fetus was diagnosed with autism. This diagnosis was confirmed three times but we prayed with them and God performed a miracle. There is nothing God cannot do!

God gave a promise to Abraham in Genesis 15:13-14.

"Then He said to Abram: "Know certainly that your descendants will be strangers in a land that is not theirs, and will serve them, and they will afflict them four hundred years. And also the nation whom they serve I will judge; afterward they shall come out with great possessions."

And He fulfilled it many generations later, as recorded in the book of Joshua:

"So the Lord gave to Israel all the land of which He had sworn to give to their fathers, and they took possession of it and dwelt in it. The Lord gave them rest all around, according to all that He had sworn to their fathers. And not a man of all their enemies stood against them; the Lord delivered all their enemies into their hand.

> *Not a word failed of any good thing which the Lord had spoken to the house of Israel. All came to pass"* (Joshua 21:43-45).

What has God spoken to your heart regarding your family, your health, and your career? Too often, the passage of time tempts us to doubt that they will come to pass. But God is ever faithful. The promise given to Abraham was fulfilled several generations later. God's promise that you and your children will be for signs and wonders shall surely come to pass. His promise for your deliverance from all troubles shall be fulfilled. His promise of supernatural provision – that you shall eat the good of the land – will be established in your life. No counsel against you shall stand. Every enemy confronting you shall be defeated!

CHAPTER 3

BIBLICAL EXAMPLES OF PROMISE FULFILLMENT

"Every word of God proves true; he is a shield to
those who take refuge in him."

(Proverbs 30:5, ESV)

Throughout the Bible, God's faithfulness to His promises
is evident in the lives of those who trusted Him, even in
the face of uncertainty, trials, and long delays. From Abraham
and Sarah's long-awaited child to Joseph's rise from slavery to
leadership, and from the Israelites' journey to the Promised
Land to David's ascension to the throne, each story reveals
a powerful truth—God's timing is perfect, and His promises
never fail. This chapter explores these biblical examples,
demonstrating that no matter how impossible a situation may
seem, God always fulfills His word in His appointed time.

ABRAHAM AND SARAH: FROM BARRENNESS TO BLESSING

The story of Abraham and Sarah represents one of the most profound examples of divine promise fulfillment in the Bible. In Genesis 21:1-2, we read: *"And the LORD visited Sarah as He had said, and the LORD did for Sarah as He had spoken. For Sarah conceived and bore Abraham a son in his old age, at the set time of which God had spoken to him."*

This fulfillment came after 25 years of waiting, during which Abraham and Sarah aged well beyond normal childbearing years. God had promised Abraham that he would become the father of many nations, but Sarah remained barren into her nineties. The birth of Isaac wasn't just a personal blessing for the elderly couple - it represented the first step in establishing the nation of Israel and fulfilled God's covenant promise to Abraham. The timing of Isaac's birth also demonstrates that divine promises operate on God's timeline rather than human expectations.

JOSEPH: FROM ADVERSITY TO AUTHORITY

Everywhere Joseph turned, it seemed circumstances were against him. Considering all he went through, it didn't look like the promise God made to him through his dreams would come to pass. Joseph's brothers tried to sink his destiny. Potiphar and his wife attempted to imprison his destiny. The butler even forgot about him, but what God had said was finally fulfilled.

It took about 17 years. Everything seemed to be working against him until his appointed time came and God's word was fulfilled. Pharaoh, the king of Egypt heard about him, sent for him, loosed him, and gave him power.

This season is your time. It is your time to be remembered. It is your time to be delivered!

Psalm 105:17-20 (KJV) narrates Joseph's transition from trials to testimonies thus:

> *"He sent a man before them, even Joseph, who was sold for a servant: ^{18} Whose feet they hurt with fetters: he was laid in iron: Until the time that his word came: the word of the LORD tried him. The king sent and loosed him; even the ruler of the people, and let him go free."*

Although Joseph was thrown into the pit by his brothers, his dream never died. When he was sold to the Midianites, his dream did not die. Even when he was lied against and imprisoned, his dream didn't die. Let nothing kill the dreams God has given you. This is your season for the divine fulfillment of those dreams, visions, and prophetic declarations over your life. God is going to bring people you have never met your way to be a blessing to you. God has you on His mind, and this is your season of manifestation

THE ISRAELITES: A MULTI-GENERATIONAL PROMISE FULFILLED

In Genesis 15:13-14, God outlined a detailed prophecy: the Israelites would be strangers in a foreign land, endure slavery and affliction for 400 years, and eventually emerge with great wealth. This prophecy was fulfilled through the Exodus from Egypt under Moses' leadership, where the Israelites left with Egyptian gold, silver, and clothing (Exodus 12:35-36).

But the promise extended beyond just the Exodus. Joshua 21:43-45 records the complete fulfillment of God's covenant regarding the Promised Land:

> *"So the Lord gave to Israel all the land of which He had sworn to give to their fathers, and they took possession of it and dwelt in it. The Lord gave them rest all around, according to all that He had sworn to their fathers. And not a man of all their enemies stood against them; the Lord delivered all their enemies into their hand. Not a word failed of any good thing which the Lord had spoken to the house of Israel. All came to pass."*

Several key aspects stand out those verses.

1. **The territorial promise was fulfilled:** *"The Lord gave to Israel all the land of which He had sworn to give to their fathers."* The conquest and settlement of Canaan completed what was promised to Abraham centuries earlier.

2. **Peace was established:** *"The Lord gave them rest all around."* This fulfilled the promise of not just possession, but peaceful habitation of the land.

3. **Military victory was achieved:** *"Not a man of all their enemies stood against them."* Despite facing numerous powerful nations, Israel prevailed through divine intervention.

4. **Every aspect of the prophecy was fulfilled:** *"Not a word failed of any good thing which the Lord had spoken."* This demonstrates God's perfect faithfulness to His promises, even across multiple generations and seemingly impossible circumstances.

Let the story of the Israelites teach you that the journey toward fulfillment may be long, but with God, arriving at the destination is assured!

DAVID: 15 YEARS IN WAITING

"David was thirty years old when he began to reign, and he reigned forty years. In Hebron he reigned over Judah seven years and six months, and in Jerusalem he reigned thirty-three years over all Israel and Judah" (2 Samuel 5:4–5).

Before David became the renowned king of Israel, he endured years of waiting and trials. His anointing as king (around the age of 15) did not immediately translate into power. Instead, what followed was 15 years of intense preparation, trials, and character development. Delays are not denials—they are opportunities to grow, learn, and prepare for a greater destiny.

God also promised David that his descendants would reign after him and that he would not lack a son to sit on the throne. *"The Lord hath sworn in truth unto David; he will not turn from it; Of the fruit of thy body will I set upon thy throne. If thy children will keep my covenant and my testimony that I shall teach them, their children shall also sit upon thy throne for evermore"* (Psalm 132:11-12, KJV).

Jeremiah 33:20-21(KJV) also affirms, *"Thus saith the* L<small>ORD</small>*; If ye can break my covenant of the day, and my covenant of the night, and that there should not be day and night in their season; Then may also my covenant be broken with David my servant, that he should not have a son to reign upon his throne; and with the Levites the priests, my ministers."*

As proof of God's faithfulness to this promise, scripture records show that:

- After David, Solomon – his son - reigned for 40 years (2 Chronicles 9:30).

- After Solomon, Rehoboam reigned. He was the son of Solomon and, therefore, David's grandson (1 Kings 14:21).

- 86 years later, Abijam (also called Abijah) reigned. He was Rehoboam's son and David's great-grandson (1 Kings 15:1-4).

- 186 years later, Jehoram, who was Abijam's great-grandson, reigned (2 Kings 8:18-19). Interestingly, even though he chose to be an evil king, God kept to the covenant He made with David.

- 313 years later, Hezekiah reigned (2 Kings 18:1-9). He was also King David's direct descendant. Indeed, the miraculous healing he enjoyed, the extension of his life by 15 years, and the preservation of the kingdom under him were also demonstrations of God's faithfulness to His covenant promise to David. 2 Kings 20:5-6 (KJV) declares, *"Turn again, and tell Hezekiah the captain of my people, Thus saith the* LORD, *the God of David thy father, I have heard thy prayer, I have seen thy tears: behold, I will heal thee: on the third day thou shalt go up unto the house of the* LORD. *And I will add unto thy days fifteen years; and I will deliver thee and this city out of the hand of the king of Assyria; and I will defend this city for mine own sake, and for my servant David's sake."*

What the above examples and countless others reveal is that God does not change, nor does He diminish in power. What He did for the people in Bible times, He is able to do for us today. As you await the fulfillment of His promises to you, do so patiently. Just like the individuals we have just considered, you will also become proof that God is faithful to His promises.

TRUST GOD'S TIMING: THERE IS A SET TIME

"For Sarah conceived and bare Abraham a son in his old age, at the set time of which God had spoken to him" (Genesis 21:2, KJV).

There was a set time for the fulfillment of God's promise to Abraham and Sarah. And it came at the exact time God said it would; it didn't come earlier or later. God operates by times and seasons. Irrespective of the happenings in the world, His timing cannot be stopped. There is a specific time—or season—for God to bring to pass the things He has planned for you.

Psalm 105:19 declares, *"Until the time that his word came to pass, the word of the Lord tested him."* This scripture describes both the time of testing and the time of fulfillment. There was a specific time for Joseph's dream from God to be fulfilled, but until that time, he was being tested and prepared.

For the fulfillment of God's promises to happen, there is usually alignment and convergence. This is a time when things line up and come together. There is an alignment of relationships, circumstances, and resources for the manifestation of the declared mandate. There is a supernatural convergence of various elements to bring about the vision God has given.

In the case of Joseph, as seen in the passage above, there was a season of testing and then there was a season of fulfillment. When Joseph's time of fulfillment came, everything began to work to make his gift shine. Pharaoh's butler and baker were sent to the same prison he was held in, and each had a dream that only Joseph could interpret. God caused happenings to make Joseph's interpretation of their dreams happen exactly as he predicted. Then Pharaoh also had a dream that no one but Joseph could interpret. Beyond interpreting Pharaoh's dream, Joseph's administrative skill shone brightly as he proffered a strategy to manage the predicted famine.

In the time of fulfillment, circumstances align so your gifts can function, making you visible and favored. In the time of preparation, your gifts are restricted and your influence is limited. However, in the season of fulfillment, the ceiling is lifted and you can function as God intends. In the time of fulfillment, you are no longer hidden. It's as if the gifts that have been there all along are suddenly "discovered" by others. This results in greater fruitfulness and expanded influence.

I don't know the situation you are currently in or what you are believing God for. Whatever it is, God will settle you with His divine fulfillment this season, in Jesus' mighty name.

WHEN FULFILLMENT SEEMS DELAYED

God's timing is a mystery that often challenges our human logic. Sometimes, the fulfillment of God's promises may seem delayed. Yet, His timing is perfect—each delay, each season of waiting, serves a divine purpose. When we accept that divine timing is beyond our control, we can rest in the assurance that every delay is part of a grand, purposeful design.

God wants me to tell you that He is not slow concerning what He promises to do in your life – He will do it at the appointed time.

> *"The Lord is not slack concerning His promise, as some count slackness"* (2 Peter 3:9a).

This scripture captivates me each time I read it. It affirms that God is an on-time God. The situations that surround us may be overwhelming and contrary, but God's WORD will never fail. Time does not affect the veracity of His counsel. If He has said it, no matter how long it takes, it cannot be denied. It took Sarah a long time but God's promise eventually came to pass.

God will fulfill everything He has promised at the set time because:

- He is dependable.
- He is reliable.
- He is not a liar.
- He is trustworthy.
- He is a covenant keeper.

I know a lady in a pastor friend's church who waited for 20 years to have a child. Twenty years isn't a joke. You can only imagine what she must have gone through during that waiting season. But at the set time, God visited her with twins! I also know another pastor friend who waited 18 years to get his breakthrough. God is too reliable to fail.

Much like the natural cycles of the earth, our lives experience seasons of preparation and harvest. The waiting period is not a sign of abandonment but a time for growth and refinement. While you're waiting, you must live in expectation and learn to step out in faith.

LIVING IN EXPECTATION AND STEPPING OUT IN FAITH

The waiting season is designed for our growth, refinement, and a deepening of our trust in God's timing. Just as a farmer does not doubt the harvest while sowing seeds, we must embrace the unseen work God is doing while we wait.

God uses our waiting season to prune, purify, and prepare us for the fulfillment of His promises. This refining process is not passive; it calls us to live in expectation, actively positioning ourselves for what God has in store.

"So also faith by itself, if it does not have works, is dead" (James 2:17, ESV).

True faith is not stagnant—it moves, acts, and prepares. Faith without action is like a lamp without oil, unable to shine when the time of fulfillment comes. Living in expectation means preparing as though God's promise is already unfolding. Noah built the ark before a single drop of rain fell (Hebrews 11:7). Abraham journeyed toward an unknown land, trusting in a promise yet unseen (Hebrews 11:8). The woman with the issue of blood reached out in faith, believing that just a touch of Jesus' garment would bring healing (Luke 8:43-48). In each case, faith was not merely belief—it was movement.

Sometimes we say we are waiting for God, whereas God is waiting for us to act. Faith is not dormant; it is active. It calls us to move forward, even when we cannot see the entire path. Peter had to step onto the water before experiencing the miracle (Matthew 14:25-29). To step out in faith is to act in alignment with God's promises, even when circumstances suggest otherwise. It requires obedience in the face of uncertainty, persistence in the face of silence, and courage in the face of fear. Like a seed buried in the soil, transformation often happens beneath the surface before a visible breakthrough occurs.

Do not mistake God's silence for His absence. Prepare actively for the blessing you're waiting for. If you are praying for a new opportunity, sharpen your skills. If you are asking for a harvest, cultivate the ground – just as Isaac did in Genesis 26:12. Take bold steps of obedience in the direction of the miracle you seek. God calls us not just to wait, but to wait well—to wait with expectation, preparation, and unwavering trust. The season of waiting is not wasted time; it is the proving ground for the promises ahead.

As you wait, live as though the breakthrough is already here. Step forward in faith, and trust that in due time, your harvest of fulfillment will come!

CHAPTER 4

HINDRANCES TO THE FULFILLMENT OF DIVINE PROMISES

"Therefore, having these promises, beloved, let us cleanse ourselves from all filthiness of the flesh and spirit, perfecting holiness in the fear of God."

(2 Corinthians 7:1)

God's promises are sure, but our positioning and response matter significantly in their manifestation. Our actions and attitudes can delay or hinder their manifestation in our lives. Let's examine the key obstacles that can prevent us from receiving what God has promised.

THE BARRIER OF SIN

Sin creates separation between us and God's promises, much like it did with Adam and Eve in the Garden of Eden. God's intention was for them to enjoy abundant life in the garden but their sin of disobedience cut their enjoyment short.

*"Behold, the LORD's hand is not shortened, That it cannot save;
Nor His ear heavy, That it cannot hear. But your iniquities have
separated you from your God; And your sins have hidden His
face from you, So that He will not hear"* (Isaiah 59:1-2).

Sin creates a big barrier between you and God; it makes your
prayers go unanswered and your efforts unrewarded.

David's sin with Bathsheba (2 Samuel 11-12) affected his
relationship with God and his enjoyment of the throne that
God had given him. Despite being "a man after God's heart",
his sin led to severe consequences. He had to flee from his
throne when Absalom, his son and Ahitophel, his trusted
advisor, revolted against him (2 Samuel 15).

Also, in 1 Samuel 2, we see how Eli's family suffered the
consequences of sin due to the rebellion and wickedness of
his sons. God had promised the house of Levi a perpetual
priesthood. However, the unrepentant nature of Eli's sons
caused them to forfeit that privilege. They all lost their lives
tragically.

Unconfessed sin can block the flow of divine promises. Regular
self-examination and repentance are the remedy. The Bible
says that God is faithful and just to forgive us if we confess
and forsake our sins (1 John 1:9).

THE TRAP OF A LACKADAISICAL ATTITUDE

Carelessness and being halfhearted in the pursuit of

fulfillment hinder God's promises. God wants us to seek Him wholeheartedly.

> *"And ye shall seek me, and find me, when ye shall search for me with all your heart"* (Jeremiah 29:13).

This passage implies that those who seek God halfheartedly will not find Him. Hebrews 11:6 also affirms that God rewards only those who diligently seek Him. A complacent spirit is marked by a casual, lukewarm attitude that dulls spiritual sensitivity. People who manifest such spirit experience a diminished awareness of God's voice and weakened connection with Him. To them, everything about God seems distant and elusive.

Christ rebuked the Laodicean church, saying:

> *"I know your deeds, that you are neither cold nor hot. I wish you were either one or the other!"* (Revelation 3:15-16, NIV).

Lukewarmness in any area of life - whether spiritual, professional, or relational - is a huge hindrance to success.

PRAYERLESSNESS: POWER MISSING

Prayer is our lifeline to heaven. Through prayer, we receive divine guidance, maintain spiritual strength, and access the promises of God. It is through prayer that we fight and win. Without regular communication with God in prayer, we are left to navigate our journey in darkness.

When you become prayerless, you become powerless, allowing the enemy to take advantage of you.

> *"For I know the thoughts that I think toward you, saith the LORD, thoughts of peace, and not of evil, to give you an expected end. Then shall ye call upon me, and ye shall go and pray unto me, and I will hearken unto you"* (Jeremiah 29:11-12, KJV).

This scripture underscores the importance of prayer. It is not enough to know that God is thinking about you or that He has good plans for you. He requires you to call upon Him. Notice that prayer is alluded to twice in the passage, showing how important it is.

If you want a fulfillment of all that God has said about you, prayerlessness is a bane you must conquer.

THE COST OF DISOBEDIENCE

> *"But Samuel replied: 'Does the Lord delight in burnt offerings and sacrifices as much as in obeying the Lord? To obey is better than sacrifice, and to heed is better than the fat of rams"* (1 Samuel 15:22, NIV).

Disobedience—whether by ignoring divine instruction or relying on our own flawed wisdom—can lead us away from our destiny. It often results in missed opportunities and a weakened spiritual walk.

Saul's disobedience cost him the throne. His kingdom could have been established and his lineage could have reigned over Israel, but his disobedience ruined everything.

Disobedience to God or to legitimate authority can cost you a lot. It can delay your fulfillment of even totally rob you of it.

Seek a heart that obeys God at all costs; it will save you from the repercussions of disobedience.

Note, very importantly, that delayed obedience is disobedience. Also, avoid the trap of selective obedience. Follow God's instructions completely.

SPIRITUAL INSTABILITY

A wavering, double-minded spirit creates inconsistency in our faith journey. This instability not only stalls spiritual maturity but also limits our capacity to receive God's blessings.

> *"But let him ask in faith, nothing wavering. For he that wavereth is like a wave of the sea driven with the wind and tossed. For let not that man think that he shall receive any thing of the Lord. A double minded man is unstable in all his ways"* (James 1:6-8, KJV).

This scripture states clearly that an unstable person cannot receive anything from God. Inconsistency robs people of both integrity and blessings.

The Israelites in the wilderness constantly wavered between faith and complaint. As a result, they missed multiple opportunities and failed to enter their rest (Hebrews 3:16-19).

Peter stepped out in faith but began to sink when he became afraid. His inconsistency in faith prevented him from walking fully in the supernatural (Matthew 14:29-30). Unstable faith makes believers ineffective in spiritual warfare and divine assignments.

THE PERIL OF PROCRASTINATION

"There is a time for everything, and a season for every activity under the heavens" (Ecclesiastes 3:1, NIV).

Procrastination can cause us to miss God's perfect timing. Delaying our response to a divine calling not only weakens our resolve but also closes doors to opportunities and blessings meant for us.

When you delay to make a call, turn in an application, or submit a proposal, you may miss out on great opportunities. If everyone around you knows you're always procrastinating, no one would trust you with important tasks. This may be a major hindrance to your breakthrough.

Like a farmer who hesitates at the moment of planting, delaying action may result in a season where conditions are no longer optimal for growth. Timely action is key to reaping a bountiful harvest.

THE ALLURE OF FALSE GODS

"No one can serve two masters... You cannot serve both God and money" (Matthew 6:24, NIV).

Modern-day idols—such as the inordinate pursuit of material wealth, career ambitions that come at the expense of spiritual growth, or unhealthy relationships—can distract us from our primary devotion to God. Divided loyalties create spiritual dissonance, impede our walk with Christ, and consequently rob us of the breakthroughs that come from regular spiritual communion.

THE PROBLEM OF INGRATITUDE

A lack of gratitude can harden our hearts and obscure the blessings God has already provided. Recognizing and celebrating past blessings will open your eyes to future opportunities and align you with divine favor.

In Luke 17:11-19, Jesus healed ten lepers, yet only one returned to express gratitude. This one man's thankful heart led to his receiving additional blessings. Gratitude positions us for more.

When we fail to appreciate what God has already done, we create barriers to receiving more of His promised blessings. Beyond that, when we fail to acknowledge His goodness, we allow a spirit of discontent and mistrust to take root, which in turn can block the fulfillment of His promises.

The Israelites in the wilderness were a prime example of ingratitude.

> *"And the people spoke against God and against Moses: 'Why have you brought us up out of Egypt to die in the wilderness? For there is no food and no water, and our soul loathes this worthless bread'"* (Numbers 21:5).

Despite receiving daily manna and other blessings, the Israelites complained every time. Their ingratitude led to delayed entry into the Promised Land, additional trials and challenges, and a loss of divine privileges. They wandered for 40 years and an entire generation missed out on the promise. Their lack of thankfulness hindered their ability to fully experience God's promise of rest and other blessings.

THE SPIRIT OF COMPLAINING

Complaining is an outward expression of inward distrust. It undermines faith and diminishes the capacity to experience God's abundance. Complaining is an expression of dissatisfaction, frustration, or rebellion against God's provision, timing, and methods. It reflects a heart that is ungrateful, impatient, or unwilling to trust God's ways. Complaining distorts perception, making past hardships seem better than God's present provision.

The most striking example of how complaining hinders the fulfillment of divine promises is seen in the Israelites' journey from Egypt to the Promised Land. Despite experiencing miraculous deliverance through the plagues, the parting of the Red Sea, and God's provision in the wilderness, they still complained.

When the ten spies returned with a negative report about Canaan, the Israelites grumbled and wished they had died in Egypt (Numbers 14:1-4). Because of their complaints and lack of faith, God declared that the entire generation (except Joshua and Caleb) would die in the wilderness and never enter the Promised Land (Numbers 14:26-30).

Their constant murmuring led to a 40-year delay in receiving the promise, and many never saw its fulfillment. Complaining hindered them from seeing God's goodness and made them unworthy of His blessings.

The scriptural injunction is that we "Do everything without grumbling or arguing" (Philippians 2:14, NIV).

Beware of a complaining heart; it will delay or block you from the fulfillment of God's promises in your life.

FEAR, DOUBT, AND UNBELIEF

Fear is the expectation of negative outcomes, rather than trusting in God's power. Doubt is wavering between faith and uncertainty about God's promises. Unbelief is outright rejection or lack of confidence in what God has said. Fear paralyzes faith; it stops believers from acting on God's promises. Doubt leads to instability; James 1:6-7 says a doubting person should not expect to receive anything from God. Unbelief can delay or forfeit blessings.

When the twelve spies were sent to scout Canaan, ten of them returned with a fearful report, saying the land was full of giants and that they were like grasshoppers in comparison. Their fear and unbelief discouraged the people, leading to rebellion and refusal to enter the land. Because of their unbelief, God swore that they would not enter the Promised Land (Numbers 14:22-23). Fear and doubt make you shrink back from receiving what God has already prepared for you.

In Luke 1:18-20, Zacharias suffered a serious consequence of unbelief. The angel Gabriel had announced that Zacharias and Elizabeth would have a son but Zacharias doubted because of their old age. Consequently, he was struck mute until the promise was fulfilled.

In Matthew 14:29-31, which we examined earlier, Peter walked on water toward Jesus, but fear caused him to sink when he saw the wind. Doubting hinders progress. Peter's faith allowed him to walk on water, but doubt made him sink.

Fear shifts focus from God to circumstances. Peter feared the storm more than he trusted the words of Jesus.

Fear, doubt, and unbelief can delay the fulfilment of God's promises or cause avoidable consequences.

IMPATIENCE WITH DIVINE TIMING

Impatience is the unwillingness to wait for God's timing, leading to actions outside of His will. It often results in shortcuts that bring long-term consequences.

Impatience can cause us to rush ahead, missing God's perfect timing for our lives. Rushing ahead of God's timing jeopardizes His promises. Cultivating patience allows us to trust in God's process, leading to better decisions and deeper spiritual preparation.

God promised Abraham a son, but because Sarah was barren and the promise seemed delayed, they acted impatiently and had a child through Hagar. That child was Ishmael, whose descendants became a constant source of conflict for Israel. Their impatience was a costly mistake that led to generational consequences and unnecessary strife, even in their immediate family (Genesis 16:1-15).

In 1 Samuel 13:13-14, Saul's impatience cost him his throne and legacy. God had commanded him to wait for Samuel to offer a sacrifice before battle. However, when Samuel delayed, Saul grew impatient and offered the sacrifice himself, disobeying God. As a result, God rejected Saul's lineage as kings, and his kingdom was given to David.

Another example is the prodigal son. He demanded his inheritance before the appointed time, spent it recklessly, and ended up in ruin (Luke 15:11-16). Shortcuts to blessings often lead to unnecessary hardship.

God's promises require waiting on His timing. As Ecclesiastes 3:11 says, God makes all things beautiful in His time!

PART 2

YOUR RESPONSIBILITY IN YOUR JOURNEY TOWARD FULFILLMENT

CHAPTER 5

EMBRACING THE FULFILLMENT OF GOD'S COVENANT PROMISES

"If you are willing and obedient, you shall eat the good of the land"

(Isaiah 1:19)

God's covenant promises are unwavering, sealed by His faithfulness, and bound by His unchanging nature. Throughout Scripture, we see His divine assurances to His people—promises of blessing, protection, redemption, and eternal life. However, to experience and enjoy these promises, you must actively embrace their fulfilment. This requires more than mere knowledge; it demands faith, obedience, patience, and alignment with God's will.

Just as Abraham believed and received, and Israel inherited their promised land through perseverance, you, too, must position yourself to walk in the fullness of God's covenant blessings. In this chapter, you will discover how to position yourself to embrace and enjoy the fulfillment of God's covenant promises in your life.

1. Surrender Your Life To Jesus

God's promises are the exclusive inheritance of His children, those who have chosen to follow Him through salvation.

> *"And if ye be Christ's, then are ye Abraham's seed, and heirs according to the promise"* (Galatians 3:29, KJV).

As a believer, you share in the covenant established through Jesus Christ. This blood covenant, sealed by His sacrifice, grants you access to the promises and blessings of God. When you surrender your life to Jesus, you gain a divine identity—your life is transformed, and your case becomes truly different. Live boldly in the knowledge that you are a covenant child of God!

> *"Christ hath redeemed us from the curse of the law, being made a curse for us: for it is written, Cursed is every one that hangs on a tree: That the blessing of Abraham might come on the Gentiles through Jesus Christ; that we might receive the promise of the Spirit through faith"* (Galatians 3:13-14, KJV).

Understanding your place in Christ unlocks a spiritual awareness that sets you apart. As a redeemed child of God, it's time to claim your covenant rights. Speak His promises over your life, walk in faith, and live the reality of His blessings.

If you have not yet received salvation, now is the time to seek the face of God. His promises are reserved for His children, and His arms are open to welcome you into the family. The privilege of God's fulfilled promises is for those who are in Christ. Are you one?

2. Locate And Personalize God's Promises For Your Life

God is committed to fulfilling only what He has promised. Therefore, you must know exactly what He has spoken concerning you. You can discover what God has said about you directly through the Holy Spirit, or through your spiritual leaders and mentors, or from the pages of the Scripture.

> *"So then faith cometh by hearing, and hearing by the word of God" (Romans 10:17, KJV)*

What you perceive from God's Word determines your perspective and experience in life. Ask God not just to help you read, but to gain newer and deeper revelations from His Word.

Whenever you hear the word of God, take hold of it and run with it. It is the pursuit of what God has promised that makes your possession a reality. So, make sure that what you are claiming is truly promised by God. It is faith when it is promised, but presumption and fantasy when it is not. Avoid stepping into situations where God has not led you. Acting based on someone else's testimony—rather than divine instruction—can lead to frustration.

Did you hear from God to buy a wedding gown when no man has proposed, or you just heard it from someone else's testimony?

> *"Who is he that saith, and it cometh to pass, when the Lord commandeth it not?"* (Lamentations 3:37, KJV).

Find out what God's Word says about your health, family and every other area of your life. There is a scriptural promise for every life situation. Locate those promises, personalize them, and stand firm in them—because if God has ordained it, He will fulfill it.

3. Believe And Accept It As The Finality

Once you have located what God is saying about you, accept it as the final authority. Circumstances around you may negate the word but they cannot override it. Let your heart and mind hold onto the word in faith.

> *"And blessed is she that believed: for there shall be a performance of those things which were told her from the Lord"* (Luke 1:45, KJV).

You ultimately become what you believe. God's greatest pain is to be doubted, and His greatest joy is to be believed.

Charles Spurgeon once said: *"Don't treat God's promises as if they were curiosities for a museum; believe and personalize them."*

Concerning the Israelites, Hebrews 4:2 says, *"…but the word which they heard did not profit them, not being mixed with faith in those who heard it"*

The Word works but if you don't believe, it cannot work for you. If there's no faith in your heart, there would be nothing for the promise to work with. We're told that Jesus did not do many miracles in Nazareth, His hometown, *"because of their lack of faith"* (Matthew 13:58).

4. Pray God's Promises To Fruition

Press for the manifestations of the promises of God on the altar of prayers.

> *"This charge I commit to you, son Timothy, according to the prophecies previously made concerning you, that by them you may wage the good warfare, having faith and a good conscience, which some having rejected, concerning the faith have suffered shipwreck"* (1 Timothy 1:18-19).

Apostle Paul laid hands on Timothy and prophesied on him. He then instructed him to wage war with the prophecies. In essence, he was asking him to pray them into fulfillment.

Don't get angry at the prosperity of others; rather, ask God for yours and He will give you. Instead of focusing on what is not working, pray over God's promises until they manifest in your life.

Sometime ago, God spoke to my wife and me during a three-day fasting and prayer. He said, "I'll roll away the reproaches of your life. I will do it one step at a time and each step will be a miracle."

At that time, we were struggling. We lived in a chalet with second-hand furniture. We had nothing, not even children. But we took that word, knelt and prayed over it fervently, again and again. And just as God promised, all the reproaches were rolled away, and each step was a miracle.

Consider also Anna and Simeon in Luke 2. They prayed persistently for the fulfillment of God's promise concerning Christ, and they lived to see it come to pass.

When you pray for the fulfillment of God's covenant promises, do so with a heart free of bitterness, grounded in faith, and rooted in a good conscience. When you pray with such a heart, the answer comes speedily.

5. Affirm God's Promises Daily And Pursue Their Fulfillment

Instead of affirming what the enemy is saying or the prevailing negative circumstances, declare and affirm God's promises daily. Declare what you believe about the promises of God over your life.

Understand that prayer is different from confession. Prayer is when you deliberately utter your desires to God, breaking barriers. Confession, on the other hand, refers to the words you speak even in unguarded moments.

Even when things seem unfavorable, continue declaring and affirming God's promises, calling those things that be not as though they were. Abram had no child when God changed his name and called him Abraham (father of nations).

God has already spoken over your life. So, what you should be talking about is not the negative news around you but what God has revealed concerning you.

> *"This is my comfort in my affliction, For Your word has given me life"* (Psalm 119:50).

Daily confessions of faith and positive affirmations are important. However, you need to also work towards the fulfillment of God's promises in your life. Affirming alone is not enough - pursue the promise!

A big proof of your faith is action. Faith without works is dead (James 2:26). If you have faith, demonstrate it by actively pursuing the fulfillment of God's promises in your life.

> *"And since we have the same spirit of faith, according to what is written, 'I believed and therefore I spoke,' we also believe and therefore speak"* (2 Corinthians 4:13).

6. Obey And Enter Into The Covenant

Keeping the conditions of the covenant is what commits God to perform on your behalf.

> *"Keep therefore the words of this covenant, and do them, that ye may prosper in all that ye do"* (Deuteronomy 29:9, KJV).

You must set yourself in alignment with God's commandments to activate His promises in your life. Obedience is the key to covenant fulfilment. Every time you fulfill your part of the covenant, you commit God's integrity to perform. The reason many people's conditions don't change is because they neglect to do their part, while expecting God to do His.

Abraham's part of the covenant was to walk blameless before God in perfect obedience (Genesis 17:1). And that is still our part today.

> *"But seek first the kingdom of God and His righteousness, and all these things shall be added to you"* (Matthew 6:33).

Service is the initiator of covenant fulfilment. If you want God's covenant promises in your life to be fulfilled, start serving God. Let the service of God be your priority. The promise is that if you put God and His righteousness first, other things will be added. When you live a life that pleases God, even your enemies will be your footstool (Psalm 110:1).

> *"And Abraham stretched forth his hand, and took the knife to slay his son. And the angel of the Lord called unto him out of heaven, and said, Abraham, Abraham: and he said, Here am I. And he said, Lay not thine hand upon the lad, neither do thou any thing unto him: for now I know that thou fearest God, seeing thou hast not withheld thy son, thine only son from me. And Abraham lifted up his eyes, and looked, and behold behind him a ram caught in a thicket by his horns: and Abraham went and took the ram, and offered him up for a burnt offering in the*

stead of his son. And Abraham called the name of that place Jehovahjireh: as it is said to this day, In the mount of the Lord it shall be seen" (Genesis 22:10-14, KJV).

Your believing is incomplete until there is active obedience. Abraham's transgenerational blessing was tested when God asked him to offer his only son. He demonstrated his faith in God by obeying even when it was hard. His faith, demonstrated through obedience, was counted to him as righteousness, leading to the fulfillment of the covenant promise.

Live a life of obedience - hear God and do whatever He asks you to do. God has great promises for you, but living contrary to His will can hinder the manifestation. May this never be your portion, in Jesus' name.

7. Keep Standing On His Promises By Faith

"Let us hold tightly without wavering to the hope we affirm, for God can be trusted to keep his promise" (Hebrews 10:23, NLT).

Rest in God's ability to perform what He has promised. Sometimes we have to wait a long time before a promise is fulfilled. Don't fret while you wait. Rest in the assurance that God will fulfill His word.

Here is another version of the above scripture verse: *"Let us hold unswervingly to the hope we profess, for he who promised is faithful"* (NIV).

Don't give up when things seem delayed. God has never failed and never will! *"You need to persevere so that when you have done the will of God, you will receive what he has promised"* (Hebrews 10:36, NIV).

That beautiful promise in verse Psalm 37:4, *"Delight yourself also in the LORD, And He shall give you the desires of your heart"* - is followed by the exhortation, *"Rest in the Lord, and wait patiently for Him..."* (verse 7).

God will give you the desires of your heart according to His will. However, sometimes you have to wait for it to come to pass. Learn to rest in God as you wait; waiting on God is never in vain.

Herbert Lockyer wrote: *"All God's promises concerning his own, are dated in heaven and with our finite knowledge we cannot read the time when many of them are to be fulfilled."* Someone also said, *"A promise is the assurance that God gives to His people so they can walk by faith...while they wait for Him to work."*

Abraham is a good example of how to wait for the fulfillment of God's promises:

> *"And being not weak in faith, he considered not his own body now dead, when he was about an hundred years old, neither yet the deadness of Sara's womb: He staggered not at the promise of God through unbelief; but was strong in faith, giving glory to God; And being fully persuaded that, what he had promised, he was able also to perform. And therefore it was imputed to him for righteousness."* (Romans 4:19-22, KJV).

According to that scripture passage:

- Abraham did not stagger at God's promises.

- He was strong in faith.

- He gave glory to God.

- He was fully persuaded that God is able.

Stay fully convinced in God's faithfulness, and He will bring His promises to pass.

8. Fight Unbelief With Every Fiber Of Your Being

Never allow any thought of unbelief to take root in your heart. Unbelief is an outright rejection of God's promise, rooted in doubt and distrust. It is a slap in God's face.

> *"How often they provoked Him in the wilderness, And grieved Him in the desert! Yes, again and again they tempted God, And limited the Holy One of Israel"* (Psalm 78:40-41).

The Israelites' refusal to believe "limited" the unlimited God. Whatever God has promised you will elude you if you don't believe. Unbelief grieves God. And it is for this reason that Hebrews 4:1-3 warns:

> *"Therefore, since a promise remains of entering His rest, let us fear lest any of you seem to have come short of it. For indeed the gospel was preached to us as well as to them; but the word which they heard did not profit them, not being mixed with faith in those who heard it. For we who have believed do enter that rest, as He has said, So I swore in My wrath, 'They shall not enter*

> *My rest,' although the works were finished from the foundation*
> *of the world."*

The works of redemption were finished from the foundation of the world but the Israelites couldn't enter into God's rest because of unbelief. Every promise of God for your life is already established and perfected in Jesus but unbelief can block you from receiving its manifestation.

It is faith at work in you that commits God to performance. Don't question how and when; trust Him, even if His instructions seem illogical. Faith is being fully persuaded of God's truth, regardless of prevailing circumstances, until His promises are fulfilled.

> *"And being fully persuaded that, what he had promised, he was*
> *able also to perform"* (Romans 4:21, KJV).

A newspaper once reported a fire in an apartment building where a little blind girl was trapped on the sixth floor while her father was at work. As the fire spread, the firemen called to the girl to jump from the window, assuring her that they would catch her in the net below. However, she would not jump and stood helplessly at the window.

One quick-thinking fireman rushed to the girl's father's workplace and brought him to the scene. As soon as the father arrived, he called out to his daughter, "It's Daddy, honey. Jump, and we will catch you." Immediately, the little girl climbed out the window and jumped into the net below, landing safely.

What made the difference? **Trust.** She knew her father would never ask her to do something that would harm her. She trusted him completely.

You must get to that point where you trust God enough to follow Him blindly. Be that person who boldly declares, "With my God, all things are possible."

Trust God even when things do not go as planned. Believe that if something doesn't work out for you, it's because God has a better way. He can never fail.

9. Consecrate Yourself To God

> *"Therefore, since we have these promises, dear friends, let us purify ourselves from everything that contaminates body and spirit, perfecting holiness out of reverence for God"* (2 Corinthians 7:1, NIV).

Make sure you are spiritually prepared to receive God's promises. Consecration means setting yourself apart entirely for God. In consecration, we surrender our will, desires and ambitions to align with God's will.

Consecration puts you in the spiritual state necessary to receive God's blessings. Throughout Scripture, consecration precedes divine intervention. For instance, before Israel's crossing of the Jordan, Joshua instructed the people: *"Consecrate yourselves, for tomorrow the LORD will do amazing things among you"* (Joshua 3:5, NIV).

Apostle Paul also exhorts in Romans 12:1-2, *"I beseech you therefore, brethren, by the mercies of God, that you present your bodies a living sacrifice, holy, acceptable to God, which is your reasonable service. And do not be conformed to this world, but be transformed by the renewing of your mind, that you may prove what is that good and acceptable and perfect will of God."*

1 Samuel 2:30 equally reveals that God honors those who honor Him. God is looking for surrendered hearts and those who are quick to confess sin.

"If I had cherished sin in my heart, the Lord would not have listened" (Psalm 66:18, NIV).

Consecrate yourself - it's a sure way to get God's attention.

10. Seek Divine Wisdom And Walk In It

You need wisdom to walk in the fulfillment of God's promises for you. Wisdom provides the insight and discernment needed to understand and properly apply God's promises to your life.

Wisdom makes fulfillment happen. It helps you discern what actions align with God's will and what might hinder the fulfillment of His promises. This enables you to make better decisions.

Joseph stepped into the fulfillment of God's promises through wisdom and discernment.

"Then Pharaoh said to Joseph, "Inasmuch as God has shown you all this, there is no one as discerning and wise as you. [40] *You shall*

be over my house, and all my people shall be ruled according to your word; only in regard to the throne will I be greater than you." And Pharaoh said to Joseph, "See, I have set you over all the land of Egypt. Then Pharaoh took his signet ring off his hand and put it on Joseph's hand; and he clothed him in garments of fine linen and put a gold chain around his neck. And he had him ride in the second chariot which he had; and they cried out before him, "Bow the knee!" So he set him over all the land of Egypt. ⁴⁴ Pharaoh also said to Joseph, "I am Pharaoh, and without your consent no man may lift his hand or foot in all the land of Egypt" (Genesis 41:39-43).

If Joseph had stood before Pharaoh and spoken foolishly, do you think the king would have made him ruler of Egypt? When you demonstrate wisdom, you'll be recommended for great positions.

Wisdom acts as a guiding light to navigate the path toward living out God's promises. It takes wisdom to be profitable in business. There is wisdom that elevates and enthrones, and there is wisdom that accelerates God's purposes for your life.

You should pray daily, asking God to saturate you with wisdom. The Word of God is the fountain of wisdom; immerse yourself in it and you'll grow in wisdom

Nothing sabotages God's promises like a lack of wisdom. God has great plans and promises for you but foolishness can delay or frustrate them.

"How much better to get wisdom than gold, to get insight rather than silver" (Proverbs 16:16, NIV).

To access the wisdom of God, you need to:

- **Fear God** (Proverbs 9:10; Job 28:28). Wisdom comes through the fear of the Lord. Those who rebel against God cannot walk in divine wisdom. The wisdom of God comes when you honor and respect Him.

- **Prioritize God** (Matthew 6:33; 22:37). Elevate the things of God above personal ambitions. Don't chase success with so much zest while giving excuses when it comes to God's work. Every empire built without God will crumble. Have a passion for God's Kingdom—if His work is struggling, it should concern you.

11. Take An Aggressive Stand Against Oppositions

Every open door comes with its share of adversaries that must be confronted and overcome. In the words of Apostle Paul, *"For a great door and effectual is opened unto me, and there are many adversaries"* (1 Corinthians 16:9, KJV).

The fulfillment of divine promises often attracts opposition, whether in the form of human resistance, satanic attacks, or systemic obstacles. These adversaries seek to hinder progress, delay breakthroughs, and frustrate God's plans. However, through faith, prayer, and decisive action, victory is assured.

Opposition to divine fulfillment in your life can be human, demonic, or circumstantial.

Human adversaries, like Herod in the Bible, position themselves as enemies of God's people and promises. King Herod saw Jesus as a threat to his rule and sought to destroy Him. Yet, God preserved His Son and removed the opposition.

> *"Now when Herod was dead, behold, an angel of the Lord appeared in a dream to Joseph in Egypt, saying, 'Arise, take the young Child and His mother, and go to the land of Israel, for those who sought the young Child's life are dead."* (Matthew 2:19-20).

Another Herod rose against the early church, persecuting believers and killing James. However, God's judgment fell upon him. *"Then immediately an angel of the Lord struck him, because he did not give glory to God. And he was eaten by worms and died. But the word of God grew and multiplied" (Acts 12:23-24).*

Beyond human opposition, spiritual forces actively work to resist believers. Ephesians 6:12 (KJV) reminds us: *"For we wrestle not against flesh and blood, but against principalities, against powers, against the rulers of the darkness of this world, against spiritual wickedness in high places."*

Satanic adversaries manifest in various ways—temptations, demonic attacks, false doctrines, and spiritual oppression. If you're not vigilant enough to engage in spiritual warfare, you will struggle to claim your God-given inheritance.

Understand that you need prayer, coupled with action. Prayer is a powerful weapon, but it must be combined with corresponding action to secure victory. Prayer brings divine intervention, but action enforces results. Faith without works is ineffective. Bold steps must accompany prayers. David didn't just pray about Goliath; he took his sling and confronted the enemy.

Victory comes when we engage in both spiritual and practical warfare. Wage spiritual warfare through prayer, fasting, and taking decisive action. Consistency in prayer and action will break every barrier.

CHAPTER 6

PREPARATION FOR EXPERIENCING DIVINE FULFILLMENT

"I will bless my people and their homes around my holy hill. And in the proper season I will send the showers they need. There will be showers of blessing."

(Ezekiel 34:26)

As far as God is concerned, all His promises for your life – both the ones already given and the ones yet to be given – are a done deal. Your focus should therefore be on your preparation for their fulfillment.

Prepared promises are meant for prepared people. The actualization of God's promises for your life requires adequate preparation.

Preparation is becoming ready for what is desired. It is the platform for the manifestation of life's opportunities. You cannot feature in a future you are not prepared for. The challenge today is that most people wait for opportunity to arise before they get prepared. This is as dangerous as a police officer loading his rifle only when he sees armed robbers. No one waits until the rainy season before roofing their house. As Smith Wigglesworth once said, "Never get ready, always live ready."

May you be consumed with the spirit of urgency and receive the grace to be prepared as you ought.

DYNAMICS OF PREPARATION

Preparation positions you for the opportunities and tasks that will launch you into your next level. It builds confidence and guarantees peace

Preparation says, "It is possible, so let's start working it now." Preparation says, "It will become simple if I take action, but it will be difficult if I neglect my part."

Proper preparation prevents poor performance. Preparation is not a gift but a choice; it is the choice of the wise.

If you don't want to be dethroned, prepare your throne. Poor preparation delivers poor results. No matter your goal, you must engage in personal preparation. You become a champion by preparation. God gives divine ability, but you must take the responsibility. Talent is worthless without preparation. The future belongs to only those who prepare adequately.

The fulfillment of God's promises in your life is a function of your preparation. I categorize these preparation into three key aspects:

- **Spiritual Preparation:** Spiritual preparation determines the results you get in the physical because the physical is controlled by the spiritual. Heart preparation determines earth manifestations. Your heart must be prepared and ready to receive what God has for you. Prepare your heart through consecration. Draw near to God and rebuild your relationship with Him.

- **Mental Preparation**: Your mind must be renewed. Your thinking must change.

- **Physical Preparation**: Your personal development must be up to date. Your skill must be topnotch. Your relationship with people must be right.

GREAT MEN ARE PREPARED MEN

"So Jotham became mighty, because he prepared his ways before the LORD his God" (2 Chronicles 27:6, KJV).

The scripture says "Jotham **became** mighty". Note the word, "became". Mighty men don't just appear; they are forged through preparation.

Although Moses was born as a chosen child to deliver the Israelites from bondage in Egypt, he spent 40 years learning the wisdom of Egypt and became mighty in words and deeds (Acts 7:22). After learning the ways of Egypt, he spent another 40 years taking lessons on service and servant leadership.

> *"Now Moses was tending the flock of Jethro his father-in-law, the priest of Midian. And he led the flock to the back of the desert, and came to Horeb, the mountain of God"* (Exodus 3:1).

There can be no greatness without preparation. Are you actively preparing for the greatness you seek?

David the king was a prepared man. His journey to becoming the king of Israel began as an apprentice tending his father's sheep. His victory over Goliath was not a lucky strike but the result of years of preparation—fighting lions and bears in the wilderness. David developed both skill and character.

Psalm 78:70-72 details the preparation process that brought David to the throne:

> *"He chose David also his servant, and took him from the sheepfolds: From following the ewes great with young he brought him to feed Jacob his people, and Israel his inheritance. So he fed them according to the integrity of his heart; and guided them by the skillfulness of his hands"* (Psalms 78:70-72).

Even our Lord Jesus was not exempt from the discipline of preparation. He spent 30 years preparing for a three-and-a-half-year ministry (Luke 3:23).

If the Lord Himself wouldn't rush into ministry and destiny, it was natural that His disciples should be prepared too. And that was exactly what happened. God's plan was to make Peter the fisherman an apostle but He did not just anoint him and send him forth immediately. Peter had to be trained, molded and transformed.

> *"And he saith unto them, follow me, and I will make you fishers of men. And they straightway left their nets, and followed him"* (Matthew 4:19-20).

Peter went through a preparation process – followership and discipleship for three and a half years. During this season of training and preparation, he was transformed from being impulsive and unstable into a bold, fearless apostle. He went from denying Christ out of fear to preaching to 3,000 souls on the day of Pentecost, performing miracles, and facing the Sanhedrin with unwavering courage.

God has promised to make you great. The question is: How prepared are you for greatness?

HOW TO PREPARE FOR GREATNESS

1. **Be focused.** Once you are specific, things will go dynamic. Distractions are side attractions designed to steal your attention and keep you in detention. Fix your eyes on the goal, knowing that distractions are only temporary. The greatest enemy of focus is distraction. *"Therefore, my beloved brethren, be steadfast, immovable, always abounding in the work of the Lord, knowing that your labor is not in vain in the Lord"* (1 Corinthians 15:58).

2. **Be persistent.** Have a never-give-up mentality. Be ready to endure till you reach the goal. *"But he that shall endure unto the end, the same shall be saved"* (Matthew 24:13, KJV).

3. **Have faith.** To be great, you must believe that God is able to help you achieve greatness. God is not moved by your emotions but by your faith. So, commit Him to perform by having unflinching faith in Him. *"But without faith it is impossible to please him: for he that cometh to God must believe that he is, and that he is a rewarder of them that diligently seek him"* (Hebrews 11:6, KJV).

4. **Make sacrifices.** You must pay the price to obtain the prize. Your preparation should be at the expense of your pleasure. *"And he said to them all, If any man will come after me, let him deny himself, and take up his cross daily, and follow me"* (Luke 9:23, KJV).

5. **Be expectant.** If you expect nothing, you will receive nothing. As you prepare adequately to achieve greatness, the omnipotence of God will be activated in your life. *"For surely there is an end; and thine expectation shall not be cut off"* (Proverbs 23:18, KJV).

FAILING TO PREPARE IS PREPARING TO FAIL

Let's take a cue from the Israelites and the Promised Land. The fulfillment of God's promise to take them to Canaan was ready from the very day they left Egypt. However, it was never actualized until 40 years later - not because God withheld it, but because the people were not ready and prepared.

This is why Hebrews 4:1-3 warns, *"Therefore, since a promise remains of entering His rest, let us fear lest any of you seem to have come short of it. For indeed the gospel was preached to us as well as to them; but the word which they heard did not profit them, not being mixed with faith in those who heard it. For we who have believed do enter that rest, as He has said: "So I swore in My wrath, They shall not enter My rest,' although the works were finished from the foundation of the world."*

Similarly, Samson was born to deliver Israel from the Philistines, but he was neither ready nor prepared for the fulfillment of his purpose. He flunked his destiny.

If you sit idly, waiting for the fulfillment of God's covenant promises over your life instead of actively preparing, you may never get it. Even if you do get it, lack of preparation will cause you to fail miserably when it matters most.

UNPREPARED VS PREPARED: THE MOSES AND JOSHUA GENERATIONS

As seen in Hebrews 4:1-3 above, the Moses generation did not experience the fulfillment of God's promise to them – *"although the works were finished from the foundation of the world."*

You must understand that the fulfillment of divine promises is not about what God will do but what God has already done that you must possess. It is by preparation that you take hold of what has been finished for you from the foundation of the world.

God commissioned Joshua as a leader because Moses and his generation did not experience the fulfillment of the promise.

73

After Moses' death, God commanded Joshua to RISE UP. To rise up means to put away whatever inhibitions or fears you have about taking action and to step forward with courage. The call is to faithfully carry out your responsibilities even in the face of extreme danger and frightening circumstances.

The Israelites were at the verge of crossing the Jordan River, but they had wandered for 40 years on an 11-day journey without any meaningful progress. However, the moment God commissioned Joshua, he commanded the people to get ready and prepare:

> *"Then Joshua commanded the officers of the people, saying, Pass through the host, and command the people, saying, Prepare you victuals; for within three days ye shall pass over this Jordan, to go in to possess the land, which the Lord your God giveth you to possess it"* (Joshua 1:10-11, KJV).

It's as though God was telling them, "I have given you the land to possess, but you must rise up and take action. You must drive out the Canaanites and the Perizzites. Take back what the enemy stole! Take back what they said is not yours!"

> *"Behold, I have set the land before you: go in and possess the land which the Lord sware unto your fathers, Abraham, Isaac, and Jacob, to give unto them and to their seed after them"* (Deuteronomy 1:8, KJV).

Unlike Moses' generation, Joshua's generation didn't fail at the task - they went in and took possession of the land.

> *"And the LORD gave unto Israel all the land which he sware to*

give unto their fathers; and they possessed it, and dwelt therein. And the LORD gave them rest round about, according to all that he sware unto their fathers: and there stood not a man of all their enemies before them; the LORD delivered all their enemies into their hand. There failed not ought of any good thing which the LORD had spoken unto the house of Israel; all came to pass" (Joshua 21:43-45).

Don't be discouraged over whatever did not work before, because that era is over. God is doing a new thing. He has promised you great things; don't stay idle, waiting for the fulfillment of those promises. Engage yourself with adequate preparation. The fulfillment of God's promises for your life requires your active participation. Joshua 21:45 did not occur without the active participation of Joshua and his generation.

WHAT DIFFERENTIATED THE JOSHUA GENERATION FROM THE MOSES GENERATION?

MOSES' GENERATION

- They were stuck in a cycle of sinning and repenting (Psalm 78:40-41).

- They were a backward-looking generation, constantly longing for their old lives (Numbers 11:5).

- They understood the acts of God but not His ways (Psalm 103:7).

- They were never challenged to know God for themselves.

JOSHUA'S GENERATION

- They were not a pampered generation. Joshua did not intercede for their sins; he confronted and allowed the offenders to be punished. The case of Achan and his household, in Joshua 7, is a good example of this. Also, in Joshua 24:14-15 (KJV), Joshua bluntly told the Israelites, *"Now therefore fear the Lord, and serve him in sincerity and in truth: and put away the gods which your fathers served on the other side of the flood, and in Egypt; and serve ye the Lord. And if it seem evil unto you to serve the Lord, choose you this day whom ye will serve; whether the gods which your fathers served that were on the other side of the flood, or the gods of the Amorites, in whose land ye dwell: but as for me and my house, we will serve the Lord."*

- They walked in conviction and consecration. *"And Joshua said unto the people, Sanctify yourselves: for tomorrow the Lord will do wonders among you"* (Joshua 3:5).

- They were a forward-looking generation, ready to possess the land.

The first thing God did in preparing Joshua and his generation was to work on their mindset. The Moses generation that perished in the wilderness without the fulfillment of the promise had a wrong mindset. But Joshua's generation moved from a season of wandering to a season of possessing the promise. They shifted from continuous disobedience to absolute obedience under Joshua's leadership.

Just as the Israelites were confronted by the giants and other enemies, when it comes to advancing your destiny, there are some Hittites, Girgashites, Amorites, Canaanites, Perizzites, Hivites and Jebusites that will stand against your becoming the person God created you to be. You must be in RIGHT standing to be able to confront and conquer them!

CHAPTER 7

THINK RIGHT WITH A MIND UPGRADE

"And do not be conformed to this world, but be transformed by the renewing of your mind, that you may prove what is that good and acceptable and perfect will of God."

(Romans 12:2)

Your thinking affects the workings of God in your life. It takes a new mind to experience a new life. Do not cross over into a new season with an old mindset. Changing location without changing your mindset may not be productive.

"And no man puts new wine into old bottles; else the new wine will burst the bottles, and be spilled, and the bottles shall perish. But new wine must be put into new bottles; and both are preserved. No man also having drunk old wine straightway desires new: for he saith, The old is better" (Luke 5:37-39, KJV).

The size of your life is determined by the size of your mind. If your mind is small, your life will be small. Until the pattern of the old is broken, it is impossible to embrace the new. Refuse to get stuck in old ways of thinking. No one rises beyond his or her level of thinking, because your thoughts create your reality.

"For as he thinketh in his heart, so is he" (Proverbs 23:7a, KJV).

Let your thinking be rooted in God's Word and His promises for your life, no matter what challenges confront you. Think scripturally, not naturally. Natural thinking is motivated by fear, controlled by feelings, and influenced by secular philosophies.

"Don't copy the behavior and customs of this world, but let God transform you into a new person by changing the way you think. Then you will know what God wants you to do, and you will know how good and pleasing and perfect his will really is" (Romans 12:2, NLT).

Your thoughts must align with the word of God. The quantity and quality of God's word in you determines the size of your mind. There were things I could not handle in the past because of my limited understanding of God's Word. But, today, I can handle such because my feeding on the Word has increased greatly.

The mindset of the Moses generation was a combination of slavery and a daily supply of manna. The Joshua generation was different; instead of waiting for manna to fall, they prepared their own provisions.

This is not a season to wait for something to happen; it's time to make things happen. If your mindset is still waiting for manna, it won't manifest in your hands. If you have the mindset of waiting for something to fall in the morning, you won't prepare your victuals. What used to work before may no longer work now.

ENGAGE IN CREATIVE THINKING

Apply Holy Spirit-inspired thoughts to create relevant solutions to the challenges of life. There is nothing that will confront you that God has not provided the solution.

> *"For who hath known the mind of the Lord, that he may instruct him? But we have the mind of Christ"* (1 Corinthians 2:16, KJV).

You have the mind of Christ – the mind behind all of creation. At redemption, you received of the creative ability of God. In other words, when you were saved, there was a mind transplant, enabling you to now share in God's infinite intelligence.

Children of God are not dummies. Rather, we are the stars the world is waiting for. So, think creatively. Regardless of how broken your environment may be, you carry within you the creative ability to reshape and redefine it.

Creativity is the ability to transcend traditional ideas, rules, patterns, and established norms to create meaningful new ideas, forms, methods, and interpretations. If one approach does not work, don't give up. Sit down with God, seek His wisdom, and receive fresh, new ideas.

ACQUIRE RELEVANT KNOWLEDGE

You cannot claim or walk in the promises of God you don't know. The word of God must work in you before it can work for you. The manifestation of God's promises is accelerated when you know them. If certain promises seem delayed or unfulfilled, the problem is not with God but with our level of understanding. We need knowledge of God's Word and how to operate its truths to walk in total freedom. The supernatural is real, and its principles must be understood to live a victorious and fulfilled life.

A successful season of preparation requires consistent study of God's Word. When things are not going well, don't just pray; seek understanding. No matter how long you pray, if you lack knowledge, things will not change. Find out where things are not working, get the right knowledge, and apply it to your situation.

Prayer is not a substitute for wisdom or knowledge; it is a complement. Daniel did not just pray; he "understood by books" and that informed his prayers and perseverance.

> *"In the first year of his reign I Daniel understood by books the number of the years, whereof the word of the Lord came to Jeremiah the prophet, that he would accomplish seventy years in the desolations of Jerusalem"* (Daniel 9:2, KJV).

Every wise person reads books and take notes. Even Jesus was not ignorant of the prophetic intentions for his life. He found His mission clearly highlighted in the Scriptures:

"And there was delivered unto him the book of the prophet Esaias. And when he had opened the book, he found the place where it was written, The Spirit of the Lord is upon me, because he hath anointed me to preach the gospel to the poor; he hath sent me to heal the brokenhearted, to preach deliverance to the captives, and recovering of sight to the blind, to set at liberty them that are bruised, And he began to say unto them, This day is this scripture fulfilled in your ears" (Luke 4:17-21, KJV).

SEEK AND OBEY INSTRUCTIONS

One major catalyst for the fulfillment of God's promises is knowing and obeying divine instructions. *"All scripture is given by inspiration of God, and is profitable for doctrine, for reproof, for correction, for instruction in righteousness: That the man of God may be perfect, thoroughly furnished unto all good works"* (2 Timothy 3:16-17).

Prayer empowers us, but studying the Word instructs us. Don't ignore prophetic instructions and divine direction.

ACT RIGHT: BOLD AND COURAGEOUS PURSUIT

God repeatedly told Joshua, *"Be strong and courageous,"* because he was about to lead the Israelites into the Promised Land - a place full of obstacles and enemies. Courage was not optional; it was essential. To step into your God-ordained destiny, you must be bold, strong, and as fearless as a lion.

"Be strong and of a good courage: for unto this people shalt thou divide for an inheritance the land, which I sware unto their fathers

to give them. Only be thou strong and very courageous, that thou mayest observe to do according to all the law, which Moses my servant commanded thee: turn not from it to the right hand or to the left, that thou mayest prosper withersoever thou goest…Have not I commanded thee? Be strong and of a good courage; be not afraid, neither be thou dismayed: for the Lord thy God is with thee whithersoever thou goest" (Joshua 1:6-9, KJV).

In demonstrating courage, observe the following:

1. **Courage is not the absence of fear but the determination to act despite fear.** It is the ability to do what you know is right, even it seems dangerous, frightening, or very difficult. To be courageous is to stand firm in truth, living out your faith in a world that often values compromise over conviction. It means sticking to godly principles, even when they are unpopular.

   God would not have told Joshua not to be afraid if fear was not a real possibility. But God assured him, *"Be not afraid, neither be thou dismayed: for the Lord thy God is with thee whithersoever thou goest "*

   Courage is trusting God's presence even in your fears. For believers, courage is not reckless bravery but confidence in God's abiding presence and power.

   "No one will be able to stand against you all the days of your life. As I was with Moses, so I will be with you; I will never leave you nor forsake you" (Joshua 1:5, NIV).

There is divine confidence and victory in God's presence. *"Yea, though I walk through the valley of the shadow of death, I will fear no evil: for thou art with me; thy rod and thy staff they comfort me"* (Psalm 23:4).

2. **Courage must be balanced with consecration.** Courage without consecration can lead to pride, and consecration without courage can lead to stagnation. The two must work together. Consecration aligns our hearts with God, while courage moves us into action.

    We must be bold, strong and firm like a lion but also as gentle and teachable like a lamb. Jesus, our Savior and Master, exemplified both; and we must follow His example.

    "And Joshua said unto the people, Sanctify yourselves: for tomorrow the Lord will do wonders among you" (Joshua 3:5, KJV).

    Access to your inheritance demands sanctification. Inheritance is only given to the sanctified (Acts 20:32). You need to decide to join the group of believers known as the sanctified.

    There is a correlation between your level of spirituality and the manifestation of God's promises in your life. There are some things God won't give us except there is spiritual maturity for handling them.

    "For bodily exercise profits a little, but godliness is profitable for all things, having promise of the life that now is and of that which is to come" (1 Timothy 4:8).

Nothing holds the dual benefits like spirituality. Every other thing ends here, except the quality of your walk with God. Spirituality essentially means:

- An undying quest to please God (John 8:29).

- A growing desire for godly living (Philippians 3:13-14).

- A faith-driven determination to live a holy life (1 Peter 1:16).

ADD DILIGENCE TO THE MIX

"Seest thou a man diligent in his business? He shall stand before kings; he shall not stand before mean men" (Proverbs 22:29, KJV).

Diligence involves competence – developing sufficient skill and knowledge to perform a task. Strive to be the best in your field and remain at the cutting edge. (Ecclesiastes 10:10). Skills become obsolete and redundant if not continuously renewed and developed.

Be diligent in planning. Praying without planning is playing. Planning without taking action is futile, action without diligence is a waste of time.

"By much slothfulness the building decayeth; and through idleness of the hands the house droppeth through" (Ecclesiastes 10:18).

Nothing works without **someone** working. Passion without pursuit produces no results. God blesses the work of your hands, not just your intentions.

SERVE RIGHT

The key to Kingdom rewards is doing Kingdom works. Open doors are rewards for Kingdom works.

> *"I know thy works: behold, I have set before thee an open door and no man can shut it…"* (Revelation 3:8, KJV).

You will struggle in life when you do not have a Kingdom dream.

> *"If they obey and serve him, they shall spend their days in prosperity, and their years in pleasures"* (Job 36:11, KJV).

SPEAK RIGHT

We live in a world that is framed and maintained by words. Your words are the building blocks of your life and your future.

> *"A man's stomach will be satisfied with the fruit of his mouth; He will be satisfied with the consequence of his words. Death and life are in the power of the tongue, And those who love it and indulge it will eat its fruit and bear the consequences of their words"* (Proverbs 18:20-21, AMP).

Be careful what you say because you have God's DNA. Open your mouth and declare only what God says about you.

There are two kinds of truth:

- Physical truth (the actual state of the matter).
- Revelation truth (what God says about the matter - 2 Corinthians 4:13).

Your mouth should be filled with revelation truth. That is how to shape your reality into what you desire.

THREE FACTS ABOUT YOUR WORDS

- Your words have creative power (Genesis 1:1-3).

- Your words are productive (Matthew 12:37). Joel 3:10 says, *"Beat your plowshares into swords and your pruninghooks into spears: let the weak say, I am strong."* That is the language of the Kingdom. Speak contrary to the negative things you see.

- Your words give assignments in the spirit realm (Numbers 14:28).

FOUR WAYS YOU SHOULD SPEAK

- Speak to God.
- Speak to the situation.
- Speak to the adversaries behind the situation.
- Speak to yourself (to your body).

Preparation puts you ahead of others. The more prepared you are, the more chances you have to enhance your performance. Preparation is the fundamental key in the school of success. You either prepare to succeed or subscribe to silent regret. Without preparation average life is guaranteed. The major cause of failure is lack of preparation, and the only chance for greatness is preparation. It's time to move into your possession of divine promises over your life. Are you prepared?

PART 3

SOME DIVINE
PROMISES FOR YOU
TO CLAIM

CHAPTER 8

THE PROMISE OF GUIDANCE

"I will instruct you (says the Lord) and guide you
along the best pathway for your life; I will advise you
and watch your progress. Don't be like a senseless
horse or mule that has to have a bit in its mouth to
keep it in line."

(Psalm 32:8-9, TLB)

Life is a series of decisions. Success or failure is the result of
the choices we make. Opportunity appeals to us, whether good
or bad. There are things that look like gold, but in reality, are
garbage. Some jobs can look very attractive but are not from
God. Your brain is inadequate to discern the many deceptions
of life. Proverbs 16:25 warns, *"There is a way that seems right to a
man, but the end thereof are the ways of death."*

There are deceptive men and women who wish to ensnare you
into dangerous relationships and partnerships. I pray for you –
anyone or anything not from God that Satan is bringing to you,
may your eyes and ears reject them, in Jesus' name.

The mistakes many have made could have been avoided if they had heard from God.

GOD DOES NOT WANT HIS CHILDREN TO GROPE IN DARKNESS

God wants to lead you where the pastures are green. As the psalmist testified:

> *"The Lord is my shepherd; I shall not want. He makes me to lie down in green pastures: he leads me beside the still waters. He restores my soul: he leads me in the paths of righteousness for his name's sake"* (Psalms 23:1-3).

God is committed to leading you where your prosperity lies.

> *"This is what the LORD says—your Redeemer, the Holy One of Israel: "I am the LORD your God, who teaches you what is best for you, who directs you in the way you should go"* (Isaiah 48:17, NIV).

Being led by the Spirit of God is of utmost importance. It beautifies your life's journey. Whenever you are led by the Spirit of God, you cannot be left behind or misled by men. **You cannot be grounded when you are guided.** The end is secured for those who are led. It is the led that will get to the end.

Laban cheated Jacob for 20 years until the day God showed him the way out. Life becomes burdensome in the absence of proper direction. The worst thing that can happen to anyone is to move fast in the wrong direction. **Direction is key to acceleration.**

WHAT IS DIVINE DIRECTION (DIVINE GPS)?

The invention of GPS has made movement from one place to another a lot easier. Before its advent, people relied on paper maps and had no way of predicting traffic conditions. But now, with the right app, you can navigate anywhere in the world.

In the journey of life, the Holy Spirit is our GPS. God gave us the Holy Spirit to provide direction. We can be led and guided by God; we can even hear His voice. As children of God, we don't have to walk in blindness. We have the confidence that we can hear His voice.

"My sheep hear My voice, and I know them, and they follow Me" (John 10:27).

Take Note Of The Following:

- Divine GPS is God's roadmap for an individual, a family or an organization. It is the ways of God revealed to men.

"He made known His ways to Moses, His acts to the children of Israel" (Psalm 103:7).

"You will show me the path of life: in Your presence is fullness of joy; at Your right hand there are pleasures forevermore" (Psalm 16:11).

- Divine direction is heaven's compass and counsel – God's leading and guidance.

FOUR DIMENSIONS OF LIGHT AND INSIGHT NEEDED FOR DIRECTION IN LIFE

1. Vision For The Future

"I will stand upon my watch and set me upon the tower, and will watch to see what he will say unto me, and what I shall answer when I am reproved" (Habakkuk 2:1-2, KJV).

This refers to God's plan and purpose for your life - His plan for you today, tomorrow and in future.

2. Direction For Daily Living

This covers practical guidance for your daily life - where to live, whom to marry (or not to marry), where to go, and when to avoid danger. Don't assume anything—seek God's counsel in everything.

"Thus saith the LORD, Stand ye in the ways, and see, and ask for the old paths, where is the good way, and walk therein, and ye shall find rest for your souls. But they said, We will not walk therein" (Jeremiah 6:16, KJV).

"Trust in the LORD with all thine heart; and lean not unto thine own understanding. In all thy ways acknowledge him, and he shall direct thy paths. Be not wise in thine own eyes: fear the LORD, and depart from evil" (Proverbs 3:5-7).

3. Revelation And Wisdom For Profitable Living

These include insights on career, business, ministry, and investments. Prayer for guidance centers around sincere inquiries: Father, should I go? Should I invest? What are the steps to take to be profitable?

David was a mighty warrior but he understood that even the mighty could fall; so he always inquired of the Lord (see, for example, 1 Samuel 30:8). Again, don't assume anything - inquire about everything!

4. Revelations Of Mysteries And Hidden Secrets

There are mysteries concerning your destiny that only God can reveal. Thankfully, He has promised to show us great and mighty things, as we seek His face.

"Call unto me, and I will answer thee, and show thee great and mighty things, which thou knowest not" (Jeremiah 33:3, KJV)

GOD'S MEANS OF GUIDING HIS CHILDREN

1. Through The Audible Voice

"My sheep hear My voice, and I know them, and they follow Me." (John 10:27)

As children of God, we don't have to walk blind. We have the confidence that we can hear His voice.

The Holy Spirit can speak to you through an **audible voice.** You see more instances of God's audible voice in the Old Testament than in the New Testament because, in the Old Testament, the realm was external rather than internal. Hearing God's audible voice is the exception, not the rule. So, don't focus on hearing the audible voice in this New Testament era, since we have the Holy Spirit within us. You don't determine how God speaks to you; He chooses the means. But rest assured—He does speak, and if you are His child, you will hear Him.

2. Through Instructions

"I will instruct you (says the Lord) and guide you along the best pathway for your life; I will advise you and watch your progress" (Psalm 32:8-9, TLB).

Instructions serve as our gateways to a life of distinction and can come in several forms:

- **Instructions through His Word**. *"O send out thy light and thy truth: let them lead me; let them bring me unto thy holy hill, and to thy tabernacles"* (Psalm 43:3, KJV). *"Thy word is a lamp unto my feet, and a light unto my path"* (Psalms 119:105).

- **Instructions through the voice of the Holy Spirit**— the inner small, yet audible voice. *"For what man knows the things of a man except the spirit of the man which is in him? Even so no one knows the things of God except the Spirit of God"* (1 Corinthians 2:11).

3. Through Wise Counsel

"Where there is no counsel, the people fall; But in the multitude of counselors there is safety" (Proverbs 11:14).

There are certain things you won't know except by divine counsel, either through your God-appointed shepherd or other Spirit-filled people. The day you begin to see your pastor as just another man, you begin to lose access to a dimension of God's guidance.

In 1 Kings 12:8, Rehoboam rejected wise counsel and He lost a major part of the kingdom. *"But Rehoboam rejected the advice the elders gave him and consulted the young men who had grown up with him and were serving him"* (NIV).

God, in Jeremiah 3:15, promises us, *"And I will give you pastors according to mine heart, which shall feed you with knowledge and understanding"* (KJV).

Don't take the words of your spiritual leader casually or get overly familiar with them. Overfamiliarity with your pastor can hinder you from hearing from God. If you stop listening to the ministers God has placed over you, you may stop hearing God in a greater dimension.

4. Through Vision/Trance – Revelation While Awake

"When there is a prophet among you, I, the LORD, reveal myself to them in visions…" (Numbers 12:6, NIV).

This usually happens when you have a consistent lifestyle of prayer. In such a moment, you are made to see with the eyes of your spirit, rather than your physical eyes. (Acts 9:8, 10-12). You could be in a semiconscious state, as between sleep and wakefulness.

You could sense a sudden detachment from your physical surroundings, as in contemplation or daydreaming. This was what happened to Peter in Acts 10:9-11. He received a symbolic vision while praying.

5. Through Dreams

"In a dream, in a vision of the night, When deep sleep falls upon men, While slumbering on their beds, Then He opens the ears of men…" (Job 33:15-16).

A dream is a series of images or events occurring during sleep. In other words, you might be sound asleep, totally unaware of your physical surroundings, and still have a vision from God. Dreams can convey spiritual messages, which may be negative or positive (Judges 7:12-15). A positive dream brings encouragement and preparation. A negative dream serves as a warning. Pharaoh's dream in Genesis 41 was a warning about an impending famine. It helped them to prepare and mitigate the effects of the famine in Egypt and the surrounding nations. Also, God used a dream to warn Mary and Joseph about Herod (Matthew 2:12-23).

Don't passively accept bad dreams. Since God has shown you ahead of time, it means you can fight and stop it. However, some negative dreams require fasting and prayer.

Note, very importantly, that you cannot rely solely on dreams for divine guidance. That's because most of your daily decisions are made while you are awake. Ecclesiastes 5:3 NLT, *"Too much activity gives you restless dreams; too many words make you a fool."*

If you are convinced that a negative dream is from God, treat it as a warning, not a final verdict. Deuteronomy 29:29 (NLT) says, *"The LORD our God has secrets known to no one. We are not accountable for them, but we and our children are accountable forever for all that he has revealed to us, so that we may obey all the terms of these instructions."*

Pray to prevent negative dreams from becoming reality. Be careful with your choices, so you don't fulfill satanic prophecies. Be especially mindful of your utterances.

6. Through His Word

"For the word of God is living and powerful, and sharper than any two-edged sword, piercing even to the division of soul and spirit…" (Hebrews 4:12).

This is God's ultimate channel for guiding His children. God's will can never contradict His Word. in other words, He will never tell you to violate what He has already stated in His Word. Whatever happens, God's Word remains eternally truthful and unchanging. Every other thing can change, except the truth of God's Word (Luke 21:33).

7. Through Circumstances/Timing

"After these things Paul departed from Athens and went to Corinth. And he found a certain Jew named Aquila, born in Pontus, who had recently come from Italy with his wife Priscilla (because Claudius had commanded all the Jews to depart from Rome); and he came to them. So, because he was of the same trade, he stayed with them and worked; for by occupation they

were tentmakers" (Acts 18:1-3).

God often orchestrates or allows situations that will spur us to take wise and strategic decisions. In the above passage, for example, Paul met Aquila and Priscilla due to circumstances beyond their control—the Roman emperor had expelled all Jews from Rome. This relationship became one of the most strategic partnerships in the book of Acts.

Note, however, that not every circumstance is ordained of God. So, it is important to apply spiritual discernment.

8. Through The Gift Of The Spirit – The Inner Witness

"For as many as are led by the Spirit of God, they are the sons of God. For ye have not received the spirit of bondage again to fear; but ye have received the Spirit of adoption, whereby we cry, Abba, Father. The Spirit itself bears witness with our spirit, that we are the children of God" (Romans 8:14-16).

When it comes to direction, many seek the spectacular and miss the supernatural by relying on prophets or external signs, like Gideon's fleece. However, there is no record in the New Testament of the apostles setting fleece before God.

It's better to trustingly leave matters in God's hands and say, "Let your will be done", instead of waiting to hear from Him through such means as "Gideon's fleece". It wasn't through someone's prophecy or some other means that you knew you were saved. Rather, it was through the inner witness of the Holy Spirit (Romans 8:16). Sometimes you can't explain it, but you just know it.

If God led you to confirm the most important decision of your life through the inward witness, then He will surely lead you in other areas.

THE NEED TO BECOME SPIRIT-CONSCIOUS

Humans are tripartite beings made up of spirit, soul and body. With our spirit, we connect with the spiritual world; with our soul, we process thoughts and emotions; and with our body, we interact with the physical world.

The implication is that, until we develop spiritual consciousness, spiritual things will be elusive to us. The more spiritually-conscious we become, the more tangible the leadings of the Lord will be to us.

Feelings are the voice of the body; reasoning is the voice of the mind; and conscience (also known as the voice of the inward man or intuition) is the voice of the spirit. If you are led by your feelings, you will be misled. Your faith must be anchored on the word of God, not emotions (Romans 8:14).

IF THERE IS NO PEACE, GOD DIDN'T SAY IT

There is peace and rest in every area of your life, when God has spoken. The absence of this peace indicates disorder and confusion – and God is never the author of confusion (1 Corinthians 14:33).

> *"And let the peace (soul harmony which comes) from Christ rule (act as umpire continually) in your hearts [deciding and settling with finality all questions that arise in your minds, in that peaceful*

state] to which as [members of Christ's] one body you were also called [to live]. And be thankful (appreciative), [giving praise to God always]." Colossians 3:15 (AMPC).

Let the peace of God be the filter; make it your judge and jury. Anything you are not at peace with, don't do it.

Philippians 4:6-7 affirms that peace is the evidence that God has spoken. *"Be anxious for nothing, but in everything by prayer and supplication, with thanksgiving, let your requests be made known to God; and the peace of God, which surpasses all understanding, will guard your hearts and minds through Christ Jesus."*

How do you know when it is the peace of God? It surpasses human understanding. Even in chaos and uncertainty, you remain unshaken—that's the peace of God.

CONDITIONS FOR GUIDANCE

1. Acknowledge God in everything.

"In everything you do, put God first, and he will direct you and crown your efforts with success" (Proverbs 3:6, TLB).

Just like you need to turn on your electronic GPS for direction, you need to connect with your divine GPS. Seek direction from God. Ask for His guidance and acknowledge Him in your decisions. This can be through a simple prayer or through prayer and fasting, depending on the severity of the decision.

God's assurance to you is: *"Ask me and I will tell you remarkable secrets you do not know about things to come"* (Jeremiah 33:3, NLT).

There are great and mighty things you don't know but need to know. Ask, and God will reveal them to you.

Moses prayed three major prayers in Exodus 33:12-18 that are very instructive:

- Lord show me the way.
- Follow me with your presence.
- Show me your glory.

There is much to emulate in these powerful requests!

2. You must be open.

Don't be set in your ways like concrete. Instead, be willing to adjust to God's instructions, even if they contradict your plans.

Christ reveals a powerful Kingdom principle in Matthew 18:3-4: *"…Verily I say unto you, Except ye be converted, and become as little children, ye shall not enter into the kingdom of heaven. Whosoever therefore shall humble himself as this little child, the same is greatest in the kingdom of heaven"* (KJV).

In Acts 10:9-18, Peter almost missed the plan of God because he was set on not preaching the gospel to the Gentiles when God was ready for it. He doubted God's instruction even after receiving a vision thrice. We must keep our hearts sensitive and tender before God, allowing Him to direct our paths, for He knows everything better than we do (2 Chronicles 16:9; Proverbs 3:5-6, 16:9).

3. Ask in faith.

When you ask, do so in faith. Once you have asked, you must completely trust God and believe that He will not mislead you.

> *"But let him ask in faith, nothing wavering. For he that wavereth is like a wave of the sea driven with the wind and tossed"* (James 1:6).

You must establish complete dependence on God by placing your trust in Him. Commit your ways to the Lord, trusting completely in His wisdom.

> *"Commit thy way unto the LORD; trust also in him; and he shall bring it to pass"* (Psalms 37:5).

When using your electronic GPS, you drive with confidence, believing that you are headed in the right direction. You're never afraid that it's taking you the wrong way. Learn to trust God's leading even more!

4. Be willing to wait for as long as it takes.

Wait patiently. God promises to lead you in His plans and purposes, but He will not necessarily reveal everything the same day you ask for leading.

> *"That ye be not slothful, but followers of them who through faith and patience inherit the promises"* (Hebrews 6:12, KJV).

5. Create a spiritually conducive atmosphere.

> *"There are, it may be, so many kinds of voices in the world, and*

none of them is without signification" (1 Corinthians 14:10).

We are a generation surrounded by many voices. Your circumstances are speaking. The economy is speaking. Your health is speaking. Your family and friends are speaking. All are crowding our minds with opinions and suggestions.

Yet, we need quietness to enjoy divine direction. Not just a quiet outer environment but much more a quiet spirit.

John 4:24 tells us that *"God is Spirit, and those who worship Him must worship in spirit and truth."* Since our fellowship with God is in the spirit, we need to create an atmosphere of quietness so that we can hear His instructions clearly (Isaiah 30:15).

Moreover, if we must enjoy constant divine direction, then praise must become our lifestyle. Psalm 22:3 reveals, *"But thou art holy, O thou that inhabits the praises of Israel."* Thus, His voice of direction will come clearly to us when we give Him the praises that His heart loves.

6. Be spiritually attuned.

You cannot operate in the carnal wavelength and expect to receive signals from the spiritual realm. Be spiritually alert.

> *"No one can know a person's thoughts except that person's own spirit, and no one can know God's thoughts except God's own Spirit"* (1 Corinthians 2:11, NLT).

You cannot live in the flesh and expect to be led by the spirit. Separate from anything that can block your spiritual reception.

Anger, bitterness, jealousy, lust, worldliness and all known sin.

In addition, a key aspect of being spiritually attuned is having continual fellowship with the Holy Spirit.

> *"As it is written: But ye have an unction from the Holy One, and ye know all things"* (1 John 2:20, KJV).

> *"Howbeit when he, the Spirit of truth, is come, he will guide you into all truth: for he shall not speak of himself; but whatsoever he shall hear, that shall he speak: and he will shew you things to come"* (John 16:13, KJV).

Know the Holy Spirit, commune with Him, and be conscious of His indwelling presence. The Holy Spirit is a Person you can talk to, ask questions, and seek help from.

7. Make Christ your shepherd through salvation.

It is vitally important you do this, if you haven't already. It is the foundation for every other blessing you will receive from Him, including continuous guidance.

> *"I am the door: by me if any man enter in, he shall be saved, and shall go in and out, and find pasture"* (John 10:9, KJV).

CHAPTER 9

THE PROMISE OF STRENGTH

"Fear not, for I am with you; Be not dismayed, for I am your God. I will strengthen you, Yes, I will help you, I will uphold you with My righteous right hand"

(Isaiah 41:10)

Strength is the ability to endure and overcome. The pursuit of life is more of a journey than a destination. And, in that journey, we engage in a fight of faith to fulfill God's plan.

Just as a jet requires fuel to fly, we need strength for the journey of life. Your success is determined by how empowered you are. The more spiritually and mentally empowered you are, the more of life's challenges you can handle.

One of the sevenfold manifestations of the Spirit upon Jesus is the Spirit of might (Isaiah 11:2). As Christians, our strength is in the Lord and in the power of His might. We can do all things through Christ who strengthens us (Philippians 4:13).

As we engage in various battles of life, we must depend on the grace of our Lord Jesus through prayer. When you're weak, you "power on" by pausing and consciously depending on the grace that is in Christ Jesus and you will be strong. Look to Jesus, draw from His strength and feel yourself getting stronger!

THE LIMITATION OF HUMAN STRENGTH

Human strength will never be adequate for facing all of life's challenges and difficulties. No matter who you are or how much willpower you have, you are still limited. You will always encounter situations in life that you just cannot manage by your human strength.

Isaiah 40:30 affirms this by saying that there are challenges that will weaken and confound even the young people that are considered embodiments of strength and agility. Our best bet therefore is the strength of the Almighty God.

> *"He will guard the feet of His saints, but the wicked shall be silent in darkness. For by strength no man shall prevail. The adversaries of the LORD shall be broken in pieces; from heaven He will thunder against them. The LORD will judge the ends of the earth. He will give strength to His king, and exalt the horn of His anointed"* (1 Samuel 2:9-10).

THE LIMITLESS CAPACITY OF GOD'S STRENGTH

"Have you not known? Have you not heard? The everlasting God, the LORD, The Creator of the ends of the earth, Neither faints nor is weary. His understanding is unsearchable. He gives

power to the weak, and to those who have no might He increases strength" (Isaiah 40:28-29).

When you leverage God as the source of your strength, you will be unstoppable and unbreakable in the journey of life. See how this works in 1 Kings 19:5-8:

> *"And as he lay and slept under a juniper tree, behold, then an angel touched him, and said unto him, Arise and eat. And he looked, and, behold, there was a cake baken on the coals, and a cruse of water at his head. And he did eat and drink, and laid him down again. And the angel of the LORD came again the second time, and touched him, and said, Arise and eat; because the journey is too great for thee.*
>
> *And he arose, and did eat and drink, and went in the strength of that meat forty days and forty nights unto Horeb the mount of God."*

People react differently whenever they lack strength for the journey of life. Depression, discouragement, confusion, or even dependency on harmful substances, such as narcotics, can result when there's little or no strength to carry on. However, the Bible assures us that *"those who wait on the LORD shall renew their strength; they shall mount up with wings like eagles, they shall run and not be weary, they shall walk and not faint"* (Isaiah 40:31).

Can you picture a person growing wings like an eagle and soaring on God's strength rather than their own limited strength? Such a person goes the distance, while others fall away in exhaustion.

We are not called to be strengthened by our human ability. Our strength does not come from how long we have been Christians, how much we know about the Bible, or how long we have been in ministry. One of the avenues for renewing our strength is through God's grace. To be victorious in life, we are to be strong in a Person called Grace—Jesus Christ. Our strength flows from our union with Him, and this strength is energized through daily communion with Him.

In other words, God gives us a strength that flows from our relationship with Jesus. Grace is released as we study His Word, commune with Him in **prayer,** and allow His Spirit to lead us. We must not depend on our own abilities but on His strength.

God's grace is the core of the gospel. Not only are we saved by grace, but we are called to grow continuously in grace (2 Peter 3:18).

God's Grace Empowers Us In Different Ways:

- **It motivates us to serve Him.** *"But by the grace of God I am what I am, and His grace toward me was not in vain; but I labored more abundantly than they all, yet not I, but the grace of God which was with me"* (1 Corinthians 15:10).

- **It sustains us in our trials.** *"And He said to me, 'My grace is sufficient for you, for My strength is made perfect in weakness.' Therefore, most gladly I will rather boast in my infirmities, that the power of Christ may rest upon me"* (2 Corinthians 12:9).

MOUNT UP LIKE AN EAGLE

"But they that wait upon the LORD shall renew their strength; they shall mount up with wings as eagles; they shall run, and not be weary; and they shall walk, and not faint" (Isaiah 40:31).

The eagle symbolizes strength. It mounts high above the earth, soaring with effortless power. The eagle is swift and sure in flight. It builds its nest in high places, on the mountains. The eagle possesses a powerful vision. It is both a mighty hunter and a fierce defender.

In fact, the F-15 Eagle fighter jet was named after the eagle because of its unmatched power as a fighter aircraft.

Power can be given, and strength can be increased. God will renew and increase your strength for the fulfillment of destiny. Waiting on God is not only about prayer and fasting but about complete dependence on Him.

Just like eagles renew their strength yearly, God calls us to spiritual renewal.

THE MOLTING STAGE: LESSONS FROM THE EAGLE

"Molting" is a time of renewal and restoration for many animals. For the eagle, each year, it undergoes this process of shedding and renewal, preparing itself for the next season. The reason it must do this is because its feathers become dull and lose their aerodynamic efficiency. Its beak also becomes dull and incapable of hunting food. Its talons lose their strength and power.

111

Therefore, the eagle must come to ground level. It humbles itself by descending to a place of rest, shedding its worn-out feathers, rubbing its beak against the rocks until a new one grows, and renewing its talons.

By the time spring comes around, the eagle has been completely rejuvenated—its feathers, beak, and talons are fully restored. It is ready to soar, hunt, and dominate the skies once again.

Isn't it a wonderful thing that when God created the eagle, He also created a renewal process? Just as the eagle regains its strength each year, we too can be renewed by God.

RENEWING YOUR STRENGTH
LIKE THE EAGLE

1. Learn To Wait On The Lord.

The secret to renewing your strength is waiting on God. Humble yourself and acknowledge your dependence on Him. Commit yourself to His guidance. Caleb, for example, gave this testimony of his life:

> *"I was forty years old when Moses the servant of the LORD sent me from Kadesh Barnea to spy out the land, and I brought back word to him as it was in my heart. Nevertheless my brethren who went up with me made the heart of the people melt, but I wholly followed the LORD my God. So Moses swore on that day, saying, Surely the land where your foot has trodden shall be your inheritance and your children's forever, because you have wholly followed the LORD my God.' And now, behold, the LORD has kept me alive, as He said, these forty-five years, ever since the*

LORD *spoke this word to Moses while Israel wandered in the wilderness; and now, here I am this day, eighty-five years old. As yet I am as strong this day as on the day that Moses sent me; just as my strength was then, so now is my strength for war, both for going out and for coming in"* (Joshua 14:7-11).

2. Seek God In Prayer And Fasting.

When you wait on the Lord, He will let you fly on eagle's wings. He will cause the wings of your destiny to stretch out. And you will mount up with uncommon strength like an eagle.

Moreover, waiting on the Lord guarantees that He will lift you above the storms of life. The eagle does not fly in the middle of the storm; it flies above the storm. Spreading its wings wide, it uses the wind that threatens to bring it down to instead go higher.

If you just stretch out on God's Word, the same wind that is trying to take you down will hold you up and drive you into the glory of God.

3. Increase In The Knowledge Of God.

"*…the people who know their God shall be strong, and carry out great exploits*" (Daniel 11:32). As you increase in the knowledge of God, you increase in strength. The more insight you gain about God, the stronger you become.

"*A wise man is strong, yea a man of knowledge increases strength*" (Proverbs 24:5, KJV).

Ignorance is still one of the deadliest weapons of the enemy (2 Corinthians 2:11). You will be limited to function in any subject you are ignorant of. Grow in grace and in the knowledge of our Lord Jesus Christ (2 Peter 3:18).

4. Savor The Joy Of God's Presence.

Learn to access and delight in God's presence continuously. Joy comes from continuously being in God's presence, and with this joy comes unlimited strength.

The psalmist declares, *"You will show me the path of life; In Your presence is fullness of joy…"* (Psalms 16:11). Nehemiah 8:10 says more about this joy of God's presence: *"Then he said to them, "Go your way, eat the fat, drink the sweet, and send portions to those for whom nothing is prepared; for this day is holy to our Lord. Do not sorrow, for the joy of the LORD is your strength."*

5. Trust In God's Faithfulness.

God will never leave us in the difficult times, but we must trust Him to give us the strength needed.

"An angel from heaven appeared to him and strengthened him" (Luke 22:43, NIV).

The angel strengthened our Lord Jesus Christ when He was in Gethsemane before the moment of accepting the cup of the Cross. Are you being persecuted for your faith in Christ? You can receive strength from His grace. Are you facing any trial, personal health issues or financial challenges? Maybe the devil is after you, trying to discourage you by throwing all kinds of darts at you: fear, anxiety, worry, concern for a wayward child, a missed opportunity, a particular failure of some kind? Hey, power on by Grace!

I pray that God will establish and strengthen your spirit, soul and body.

CHAPTER 10

THE PROMISE OF PROVISION

"And my God shall supply all your need according to
His riches in glory by Christ Jesus"

(Philippians 4:19)

S alvation in Christ is a call into a life of supernatural provision
and abundance.

By redemption, we have a covenant right to live the abundant
life.

> *"The thief comes only in order to steal and kill and destroy. I
> came that they may have and enjoy life, and have it in abundance
> (to the full, till it overflows)"* (John 10:10, AMP)

Our God is the Almighty, the El Shaddai. He is the God who
is more than enough. In the Hebrew tongue, the meaning of
"El Shaddai" is "the all-breasted God" – that is, the God who
nourishes, supplies and satisfies in abundance. He is the all-
sufficient sustainer who abundantly blesses with all manner

of blessings. Everything God does is over the top, in surplus, super-abundant, overflowing, good measure, pressed down, shaken together and running over!

THE TABLE IS SET

In Psalm 23:5, David says, *"You [the Lord] prepare a table before me in the presence of my enemies…"*

Just like earthly shepherds provide for their sheep, God, our great Shepherd guarantees supernatural supplies and abundance. *"I am the good shepherd: the good shepherd giveth his life for the sheep"* (John 10:11, KJV).

And there is only one guest at this table of abundant provision – **YOU.** The table is set for all your needs - your health, your finance, your future, your daily living.

In Bible days, there were mountainous places where lush, green pastures flourished, providing good and healthy grass for sheep to graze. These areas were known as "tablelands." The shepherd would first prepare the land by removing poisonous grasses and flowers that could harm the sheep. Thereafter, they led the sheep to have their fill of nutritious pasture.

Generally, when it comes to provision, there are four levels of sufficiency:

1. Barely enough.

This is the level of barely surviving and not knowing where the next provision will come from. Those at this level struggle to enjoy even the necessities of life.

2. Just enough.

This is a life where you have just what you need at any given time – no more, no less. It is the place of sufficiency, where one has just enough.

> *"And God is able to provide you with every blessing in abundance, so that you may always have enough of everything and may provide in abundance for every good work"* (2 Corinthians 9:8, RSV).

Although this level is an improvement over "barely enough", it's still not God's best for us. Why? Because, at this level, you will hardly be able to bless others.

3. More Than Enough.

This is the level where you are not only able to meet your needs but also have an overflow to help others.

> *"And they did all eat, and were filled: and they took up of the fragments that remained twelve baskets full"* (Matthew 14:20).

Here, the story of the five loaves and two fish reveals the divine pattern of supply—from lack to sufficiency, and ultimately, to surplus.

4. Forever Enough.

This is God's ultimate level of provision— a state of inexhaustible, unending supernatural flow. It is the place of perpetual and permanent divine provision, a covenantal abundance that transcends generations.

This is where God wants us to be. Here, the overflow of His blessings continues beyond an individual's lifetime.

> *"And I will make my covenant between me and thee, and will multiply thee exceedingly. And Abram fell on his face: and God talked with him, saying, As for me, behold, my covenant is with thee, and thou shalt be a father of many nations. Neither shall thy name any more be called Abram, but thy name shall be Abraham; for a father of many nations have I made thee. And I will make thee exceeding fruitful, and I will make nations of thee, and kings shall come out of thee. And I will establish my covenant between me and thee and thy seed after thee in their generations for an everlasting covenant, to be a God unto thee, and to thy seed after thee"* (Genesis 17:2-7).

WALKING IN SUPERNATURAL ABUNDANCE

The root word for "abundance" is "abound". "Abound" comes from two words: "a" and "bound." "Bound" means restricted, limited, or confined. "A" means "not" or "without." So, "abound" means "without limitations."

Walking in supernatural abundance means operating in the realm of unlimited supply, enjoying the boundless resources of God's grace. Anything man-made is limited, it always comes to an end. But God's supernatural abundance is inexhaustible.

We see an example of the manifestation of divine abundance in 2 Kings 7:8-10.

> *"When the men with leprosy arrived at the edge of the camp, they went into one tent after another, eating and drinking wine; and*

they carried off silver and gold and clothing and hid it. Finally, they said to each other, "This is not right. This is a day of good news, and we aren't sharing it with anyone! If we wait until morning, some calamity will certainly fall upon us. Come on, let's go back and tell the people at the palace." So they went back to the city and told the gatekeepers what had happened. "We went out to the Aramean camp," they said, "and no one was there! The horses and donkeys were tethered and the tents were all in order, but there wasn't a single person around!" (2 Kings 7:8-10, NLT).

One of the couples in our ministry gave their testimony not long ago. God lifted them from a life of struggle into a life of abundance. When they joined the ministry, they were barely surviving, but when they shared their testimony, they were employing 56 people!

Living in abundance is not about having a fleet of cars, houses, or material possessions. It is not about how much money you have, but about a continuous supply, flowing from your covenant with God.

Here is Philippians 4:19 again, *"But my God shall supply all your need according to his riches in glory by Christ Jesus."*

Observe that it says *"according to his riches in glory by Christ Jesus"*, not according to your bank account or the lucrativeness of your job. As good as your careers or bank accounts may be, they are all subject to change. Your career, business, and savings— all these have their place, but they are subject to economic conditions and financial limitations. Believers are meant to live according to the riches of God's Kingdom.

Abraham enjoyed supernatural abundance on the platform of the covenant (Genesis 12:1-3). God had called and commanded him (when he was still known as Abram) to leave his country. He obeyed, yet he encountered famine. But despite the famine, Abraham prospered.

> *"And Abram was very rich in cattle, in silver and in gold"* (Genesis 13:2, KJV).

Abraham's wealth was supernatural and transgenerational. His descendants (the Israelites) walked into abundance because of God's covenant with him.

> *"He brought them forth also with silver and gold and there was not one feeble person among their tribes"* (Psalm 105:37, KJV).

Covenant changes your status when you enter into it. Your life becomes mixed with the person or entity you are in covenant with. A divine covenant is a divine exchange. It transforms your life and links you to God's unlimited provision. The covenant gave Abraham a wealth zone, which included livestock, silver and gold.

UNLIMITED ACCESS

One of the greatest blessings of our connection with God as our Shepherd is access to supernatural supply. We live in a world where hardships are real, where difficult times are undeniable—yet, so is God's ability to provide supernaturally.

"They shall not be ashamed in the evil time: and in the days of famine, they shall be satisfied." (Psalms 37:19)

"If they obey and serve Him, they shall spend their days in prosperity, and their years in pleasures." (Job 36:11)

According to Scripture, the supernatural is not meant to be an occasional experience for believers—it is supposed to be our natural way of life.

"The wind blows wherever it pleases. You hear its sound, but you cannot tell where it comes from or where it is going. So it is with everyone born of the Spirit." (John 3:8)

As born-again believers, we are designed to live supernaturally. This is God's expectation for His children. Functioning in the supernatural should be the believer's default setting. God has already orchestrated divine means to meet our needs, but the challenge lies in our ability to embrace and operate in this reality.

We have been trained in the natural all our lives; therefore, to walk in supernatural provision, we must be retrained in the supernatural. It takes a renewed mind to live a renewed life.

"Do not be conformed to this world, but be transformed by the renewing of your mind…" (Romans 12:2)

Supernatural supply begins with a supernatural mindset. Until we develop a consciousness of God's divine economy, we will struggle to access it. To enjoy God's supernatural agenda, we must first believe in it.

SCRIPTURAL VALIDATION OF SUPERNATURAL SUPPLY

When the children of Israel came out of Egypt, God took charge and fed them two full meals for forty years (Exodus 16:8). Imagine that - two full meals daily in the wilderness! God knows how to provide for His people even in the wilderness.

> *"The Israelites ate manna forty years, until they came to a land that was settled; they ate manna until they reached the border of Canaan"* (Exodus 16:35, NIV).

About three million people eating twice daily for 40 years! That's supernatural provision on an unimaginable scale.

Elijah also enjoyed supernatural supply. The Lord gave Elijah specific instructions and he was supplied with food morning and evening.

> *"And Elijah the Tishbite, who was of the inhabitants of Gilead, said unto Ahab, As the Lord God of Israel liveth, before whom I stand, there shall not be dew nor rain these years, but according to my word.* [2] *And the word of the Lord came unto him, saying, Get thee hence, and turn thee eastward, and hide thyself by the brook Cherith, that is before Jordan. And it shall be, that thou shalt drink of the brook; and I have commanded the ravens to feed thee there"* (1 Kings 17:1-4, KJV).

> *"And he looked, and, behold, there was a cake baken on the coals, and a cruse of water at his head. And he did eat and drink, and laid him down again. And the angel of the LORD came again the second time, and touched him, and said, Arise and eat;*

because the journey is too great for thee. And he arose, and did eat and drink, and went in the strength of that meat forty days and forty nights unto Horeb the mount of God." (1 Kings 19:6-8).

Other examples of supernatural supply include:

- The widow who was in despair (2 Kings 4:1-7).
- The feeding of the five thousand (John 6:10-13).
- The coin from the mouth of the fish (Matthew 17:24-27).

God knows how to get you what you require. Leave the method to God. Your task is to simply follow His supernatural command.

DECISIONS THAT WILL LINK YOU WITH GOD'S SUPERNATURAL ABUNDANCE

1. Decide to put God first.

"But thou shalt remember the Lord thy God: for it is He that giveth thee power to get wealth…" (Deuteronomy 8:18, KJV).

To avoid making a shipwreck of your destiny, it is not just sufficient to start the year with God—it is essential to put God first throughout the year. When you put God first, He ensures that the resources of heaven are made available to you first. When you make God your pursuit, good things will pursue you in all your endeavors.

Jesus, our perfect example, put His Father first. Long before dawn, He would wake up and commune with His Father until daybreak. This was the secret of His power. When you spend enough time in God's presence, you will carry His anointing, which will overflow and touch lives.

When you wake up in the morning, acknowledge God. Give Him your first fruit—not just financially, but in your priorities. First fruit is not limited to money; it is about where you place God in your world. Align yourself with Him.

> *"That thou shalt take of the first of all the fruit of the earth, which thou shalt bring of thy land that the LORD thy God giveth thee, and shalt put it in a basket, and shalt go unto the place which the LORD thy God shall choose to place His name there"* (Deuteronomy 26:2).

2. Decide to let God lead you.

> *"The Lord is my shepherd; I shall not want. He maketh me to lie down in green pastures: he leadeth me beside the still waters"* (Psalms 23:1-2, KJV).

Your supplies are in God's leading; wherever He leads is where His grace follows.

There is a place of prepared blessing. *"And I will give thee the treasures of darkness, and hidden riches of secret places, that thou mayest know that I, the LORD, which call thee by thy name, am the God of Israel"* (Isaiah 45:3, KJV).

You cannot be grounded when you are guided. It is said of Rockefeller that he was to buy the famous ship known as the *Titanic*. However, as a Christian, he prayed and wasn't led to proceed with the purchase.

How did the lepers in 2 Kings 7 get into abundance? They stepped out on the declared word. This is a season to trust God's word and step out in faith.

Opportunity does not always equal divine guidance. Not every open door is God's door. Not all opportunities are good doors.

Even Jesus rejected certain opportunities. Following the feeding of the five thousand, some people wanted to make Him king but He declined (John 6:14-15). At another time, He was pressured to publicize Himself but He refused:

> *"Now the Jews' Feast of Tabernacles was at hand. His brothers therefore said to Him, "Depart from here and go into Judea, that Your disciples also may see the works that You are doing. For no one does anything in secret while he himself seeks to be known openly. If You do these things, show Yourself to the world." For even His brothers did not believe in Him. Then Jesus said to them, "My time has not yet come, but your time is always ready. The world cannot hate you, but it hates Me because I testify of it that its works are evil. You go up to this feast. I am not yet going up to this feast, for My time has not yet fully come." When He had said these things to them, He remained in Galilee"* (John 7:2-9).

Christ revealed that His time hadn't yet fully come. And, indeed, when His time finally came, He was announced. Following God's guidance is what announces a person's destiny and ministry, not desperation or cutting corners.

3. Decide to be diligent.

"He who has a slack hand becomes poor, But the hand of the diligent makes rich" (Proverbs 10:4).

Nothing works unless someone puts in the work. The world sells the illusion of success without effort. But true abundance and success require diligence.God is committed to blessing the work of our hands. Diligence is work directed toward the proper channel.

Proverbs 12:27 in the Amplified Bible says: *"The lazy man does not catch and roast his prey, but the precious possession of a [wise] man is diligence* [because he recognizes opportunities and seizes them]."

Diligence is the wise man's greatest asset. It means investing your abilities, strength, and all you have into the pursuit of your destiny or kingdom assignment. Success demands work.

4. Decide to be disciplined.

"A person without self-control is like a city with broken-down walls" (Proverbs 25:28).

The covenant of supernatural abundance requires discipline.

Self-discipline distinguishes you. It is the bridge between your goals and achievement. To be disciplined is to impose necessary restrictions on yourself willingly—so you won't have them imposed on you forcefully.

Discipline is the control valve of destiny. How far a life will go is determined by how disciplined that life is. Discipline is the capacity to restrain desire and delay gratification. It is being able to distinguish between the lawful and expedient. Not everything that is available is necessary. (1 Corinthians 6:12).

You need discipline in the following areas:

- **Time management** – Time is currency. You can spend or invest it. Investing time upgrades destiny; wasting time downgrades it (Psalm 90:12).

- **Taste control** – Not everything is for you (Proverbs 23:1-2).

- **Thought control** – Your mind is the engine room of your life. (Proverbs 4:23; Philippians 4:8; 2 Corinthians 10:5).

- **Speech discipline** – Speak right, and your life will go right (1 Peter 3:10).

- **Financial discipline** – A wise person does not spend everything he or she has (Proverbs 10:4).

- **Association control** – Wrong company destroys destiny (Proverbs 13:20; 1 Corinthians 15:33).

5. **Decide to walk in the fullness of the power of the Holy Spirit.**

"The wind blows where it wishes, and you hear the sound of it, but cannot tell where it comes from and where it goes. So is everyone who is born of the Spirit" (John 3:8).

The Christian life is inherently supernatural and can only be fully lived through the power of the Holy Ghost. Supernatural results require supernatural power. In this world full of wickedness, unpredictable twists and turns, and unforeseen circumstances, we would be doomed without the daily empowerment of the Holy Spirit.

The Holy Spirit alerts us to and diverts us from dangers ahead. He reveals future events and knows the outcome of any project before it even begins. He also grants the power of discernment.

Through the power of the Holy Ghost, we see in Acts 16:16-18 how Apostle Paul cast out the demonic spirit in a certain damsel who had the gift of divination and profited her master through soothsaying. Although she praised Paul and other ministers, declaring that they were servants of the Most High God who preached the way of salvation, Paul discerned that the spirit in her was not of God. He saw beyond her words and recognized her true intentions.

When a demonic agent disguises as a man of God, trying to deceive you by revealing hidden details of your life (things only you should know), you need the Spirit of God to discern the deception.

The Holy Spirit also helps us conquer temptation. He is not a luxury for a select few but a necessity for every believer. He is not reserved for ministers alone. It is crucial to seek God's Spirit so that the devil and his agents are subdued under your feet.

The Holy Spirit empowers us to be bold witnesses and leads

us into abundance. It was not merely an ordinary act for four lepers to plunder an entire nation in 2 Kings 7 without even drawing a sword—that was a supernatural intervention. Likewise, multiplying a little boy's lunch to feed five thousand was not ordinary but a manifestation of the Holy Spirit's power.

As a businessperson, you need the Holy Spirit to close your deals. You need Him to flourish in all you do.

"However, when He, the Spirit of truth, has come, He will guide you into all truth; for He will not speak on His own authority, but whatever He hears He will speak; and He will tell you things to come. He will glorify Me, for He will take of what is Mine and declare it to you. All things that the Father has are Mine. Therefore I said that He]will take of Mine and declare it to you" (John 16:13-15).

6. Decide To Be Committed To The Law Of Seedtime And Harvest.

Everything in life is subject to the law of seedtime and harvest. Your word, prayer, action, service, smile and so on are all seeds. If you sow sparingly, you will reap sparingly but if you sow bountifully, you will reap bountifully.

What are you expecting God to do for you? Begin to sow prayer into it; speak and confess into it and press into it by sacrificial giving. If you want God to move mightily, especially for financial breakthrough, learn to sow; increase your seeding and make sure you do it with joy and not out of compulsion.

When you release your seed, you schedule a harvest. This is how to change season. If you want to change your season of poverty, scarcity and lack, you cannot run away from the power of the seed. Every seed is coded with an instruction to produce (Genesis 8:22; Galatians 6:7).

7. Decide To Be A Soul Winner.

God has a burden for the lost. When you align with His heartbeat, you position yourself for supernatural favor. When you take delight in heaven's agenda, God will take delight in making you prosperous.

"Let them shout for joy, and be glad, that favor my righteous cause: yea, let them say continually, Let the Lord be magnified, which hath pleasure in the prosperity of his servant" (Psalm 35:27, KJV).

Divine favor is a reward for championing God's agenda.

"Thou shalt arise, and have mercy upon Zion: for the time to favor her, yea, the set time, is come. For thy servants take pleasure in her stones, and favor the dust thereof" (Psalm 102:13-14, KJV).

"And they that be wise shall shine as the brightness of the firmament; and they that turn many to righteousness as the stars for ever and ever" (Daniel 12:3).

Do you want heaven's favor? Do you desire prosperity without adversity? Win souls. God prioritizes prayers from those committed to His Kingdom agenda.

8. Decide To Walk In Obedience.

One of the most vital channels through which we gain access to the supplies of heaven is obedience. No one gains access to overflowing blessings without committed obedience. Kingdom blessings are not random; they are conditional. Obedience is the trigger that provokes heaven's release.

It may not always be convenient. It may stretch you. But obedience is the key to lasting comfort.

"If ye be willing and obedient, ye shall eat the good of the land" (Isaiah 1:19).

9. Decide To Be Committed To Tithing.

"Bring all the tithes into the storehouse, that there may be food in My house, and try Me now in this," says the Lord of hosts, "if I will not open for you the windows of heaven and pour out for you such blessing that there will not be room enough to receive it" (Malachi 3:10-11).

Tithing secures your portion in God's provision. It is God's portion that ensures you don't lose your own portion.

"Here mortal men receive tithes, but there He receives them, of whom it is witnessed that He lives" (Hebrews 7:8).

The tithe is the key that unlocks your heritage of supplies from above. When you give your tithe, it is received in heaven and unlocks your heritage of wealth.

In the natural world, the process that produces rainfall is evaporation first and then condensation. Our giving is like vapor. It is the engagement of the tithing that opens our heaven and causes that which it is pregnant with to fall upon the earth. Recall again that everything in life is subject to the law of seedtime and harvest.

10. Decide To Engage The Force Of Faith.

Faith is a non-negotiable force in unlocking supernatural supply.

"Blessed is she who believed, for there will be a fulfillment of those things which were told her from the Lord" (Luke 1:45).

Be absolutely assured that the covenant cannot fail. Everything in God's Kingdom answers to faith. Where faith is absent, the connection is broken. Our access to divine resources is directly linked to our faith.

"Let us therefore come boldly to the throne of grace, that we may obtain mercy and find grace to help in time of need" (Hebrews 4:16).

You have to learn to trust God daily to fulfil his words. Take faith steps. Establish your complete dependency on him by placing your trust in Him.

"My God shall supply your need according to His riches in glory…" (Philippians 4:19).

As our Shepherd, God longs to meet our needs but He wants us to establish complete dependence upon Him. Just as a sheep fully trusts its shepherd, we must completely trust God for our provision.

"Trust in the Lord with all your heart, and lean not on your own understanding; in all your ways acknowledge Him, and He shall direct your paths" (Proverbs 3:5-6).

WHY YOU NEED SUPERNATURAL ABUNDANCE

1. That You May Be A Blessing.

"Now the LORD had said unto Abram, Get thee out of thy country, and from thy kindred, and from thy father's house, unto a land that I will shew thee: And I will make of thee a great nation, and I will bless thee, and make thy name great; and thou shalt be a blessing." (Genesis 12:1-2, KJV).

Supernatural abundance is not just for personal comfort—it positions you as a conduit of God's blessings to others. When you walk in divine provision, you become a solution provider, an agent of good works in the Kingdom.

Like Dorcas, whose generosity impacted many (Acts 9:36-39), you will have the capacity to help the needy, support ministries, and extend God's love through giving.

"God can bless you with everything you need, and you will always have more than enough to do all kinds of good things for others"
(2 Corinthians 9:8, CEV)

Abundance is not about hoarding wealth; it is about distribution. When you give, God empowers you for greater increase.

2. To Establish And Validate The Covenant.

"But thou shalt remember the LORD thy God: for it is he that giveth thee power to get wealth, that he may establish his covenant which he sware unto thy fathers, as it is this day"
(Deuteronomy 8:18)

Your divine abundance is a testament to the reality of God's covenant. When you walk in supernatural provision, you demonstrate the fulfillment of God's promises to Abraham and his descendants.

Every covenant has tokens of proof. Divine abundance is one of the evidences that you are in alignment with God's covenant blessings.

3. To Promote The Gospel Of The Kingdom.

"Cry yet, saying, Thus saith the LORD of hosts; My cities through prosperity shall yet be spread abroad; and the LORD shall yet comfort Zion, and shall yet choose Jerusalem" (Zechariah 1:17, KJV).

The advancement of God's Kingdom requires resources. One of the ways the gospel spreads across the earth is through the generosity of God's people.

Consider Luke 7:5, where the centurion built a synagogue for the Jews. You cannot build when you are poor. A financially empowered believer can sponsor missions, support churches, and ensure the gospel reaches the nations.

Wealth in the hands of the righteous accelerates the fulfillment of God's purpose on earth.

God wants His people to prosper because prosperity fuels purpose. When you embrace this truth, you position yourself for a life of impact, generosity, and divine fulfillment.

CHAPTER 11

THE PROMISE OF FRUITFULNESS

"I will look on you with favor and make you fruitful
and increase your numbers, and I will keep my
covenant with you."

(Leviticus 26:9, NIV)

This is your season of covenant fulfillment, and one way
this will be manifested is through the blessing of all-round
fruitfulness. God is a covenant-keeping God. He packages His
promises within a covenant. Through the covenant process,
God binds not only man but also Himself.

What makes a covenant different from a promise is that it is
backed up by an oath.

As Hebrews 6:13-18 reveals, *'For when God made promise to
Abraham, because he could swear by no greater, he sware by himself,
Saying, Surely blessing I will bless thee, and multiplying I will multiply
thee. And so, after he had patiently endured, he obtained the promise. For
men verily swear by the greater: and an oath for confirmation is to them*

an end of all strife. Wherein God, willing more abundantly to shew unto the heirs of promise the immutability of his counsel, confirmed it by an oath: That by two immutable things, in which it was impossible for God to lie, we might have a strong consolation, who have fled for refuge to lay hold upon the hope set before us" (KJV).

By covenant, you have a divine mandate to be fruitful.

God has a covenant of fruitfulness with His children (Genesis 1:28). It is part of our inheritance in Christ. God did not create you to be stagnant or fruitless. In other words, living a life of barrenness is anti-covenant!

> *Barrenness and fruitlessness contradict the first blessing God spoke over mankind: "And God blessed them, and God said unto them, Be fruitful, and multiply, and replenish the earth, and subdue it: and have dominion over the fish of the sea, and over the fowl of the air, and over every living thing that moveth upon the earth"* (Genesis 1:28).

Fruitfulness was the first creational blessing invoked upon man.

> *A child of a baker is not meant to beg for bread. Likewise, every child of God is ordained to be fruitful. Fruitfulness is part of our reward for service. Exodus 23:25-26. Every serving child of God is entitled to rewards. "Thou shalt be blessed above all people: there shall not be male or female barren among you, or among your cattle"* (Deuteronomy 7:14, KJV).

DIMENSIONS OF FRUITFULNESS

To be fruitful means to grow, flourish, and be productive. It means to blossom and yield increase. After creating Adam and Eve, God blessed them, and everything else became the initiative of Adam and Eve and no more that of God.

Fruitfulness is not limited to child-bearing. God has ordained fruitfulness in every area of our lives. To be fruitful is to be innovative. It is to demonstrate all-rounded life productivity. This means productivity in not just in one or two areas but in every area, and all through your life. God wants you to excel spiritually, intellectually, physically, biologically, and financially.

"Blessed shall be the fruit of your body, the produce of your ground and the increase of your herds, the increase of your cattle and the offspring of your flocks. "Blessed shall be your basket and your kneading bowl. "Blessed shall you be when you come in, and blessed shall you be when you go out" (Deuteronomy 28:4-6).

THE FRUITS YOU MUST BEAR

1. The fruit of your body.

This refers to bodily productivity—fertility, health, and generational increase. One dimension of the creational blessing is the grace to populate the earth. This includes the right to marry and produce godly offspring who will, in turn, raise godly generations.

"Lo, children are an heritage of the Lord: and the fruit of the womb is his reward. ⁴ As arrows are in the hand of a mighty man; so are children of the youth." (Psalm 127: 3-4, KJV).

Barrenness was a result of the curse (Deuteronomy 28:18). But Jesus terminated the curse and reconnected us to the blessing. Some experience barrenness in childbearing, while others struggle to find a life partner. Don't buy into the world's lie that marriage and children are unnecessary.

"Blessed is every one that fears the Lord; that walketh in his ways. ² For thou shalt eat the labor of thine hands: happy shalt thou be, and it shall be well with thee. ³ Thy wife shall be as a fruitful vine by the sides of thine house: thy children like olive plants round about thy table. ⁴ Behold, that thus shall the man be blessed that fears the Lord. ⁵ The Lord shall bless thee out of Zion: and thou shalt see the good of Jerusalem all the days of thy life. ⁶ Yea, thou shalt see thy children's children, and peace upon Israel" (Psalm 128:1-6, KJV).

The NLT puts it even more clearly: *"How joyful are those who fear he Lord— all who follow his ways! You will enjoy the fruit of your labor. How joyful and prosperous you will be! Your wife will be like a fruitful grapevine, flourishing within your home. Your children will be like vigorous young olive trees as they sit around your table. That is the Lord's blessing for those who fear him. May the Lord continually bless you from Zion. May you see Jerusalem prosper as long as you live. May you live to enjoy your grandchildren..."*

As a confirmation of God's faithfulness to the promise of unending bodily fruitfulness for His people, it is recorded of Elisabeth, mother of John the Baptist:

> *"And, behold, thy cousin Elisabeth, she hath also conceived a son in her old age: and this is the sixth month with her, who was called barren. For with God nothing shall be impossible"* (Luke 1:36-37).

2. The fruit of the mind: ideas.

It is equally God's desire that you abound in the fruit of your mind. Your mind is a treasure, a powerhouse of ideas and innovations, that must not be wasted on idleness or negativity.

> *"Hear, O earth: behold, I will bring evil upon this people, even the fruit of their thoughts, because they have not hearkened unto my words, nor to my law, but rejected it"* (Jeremiah 6:19, KJV).

When God made Adam, He didn't give him ready-made tools— no bed, no soap, no knife. He simply commanded him to "Be fruitful." Adam engaged his mind and created everything he needed.

By Genesis 4—only seven generations after Adam—humanity had already developed methods to raise livestock, manufacture musical instruments, and forge tools from iron and bronze.

How did they achieve so much without formal education? Job 32: 8 gives us an insight: *"But there is a spirit in man and the breath of the Almighty gives him understanding."*

This proves that a lack of education is never an excuse for fruitlessness. As a child of God, you have the mind of Christ. You are creative, innovative, and capable of transforming the world through consecrated and anointed ideas. There is an idea in you the world is craving for – only by activating it will you become an unstoppable force. *"And the LORD said, Behold, the people is one, and they have all one language; and this they begin to do: and now nothing will be restrained from them, which they have imagined to do"* (Genesis 11:6, KJV)

Your mind determines your destiny. Therefore, feed your mind with productive thoughts.

> *"How precious also are thy thoughts unto me, O God! how great is the sum of them!"* Psalm 139:17

To change your life, you must change the way you think. Every action begins with a thought. Behind every behavior is a belief, and behind every belief is a mindset that shapes your life.

Long before psychologists understood this principle, God had already revealed it: *"Be careful how you think; your life is shaped by your thoughts"* (Proverbs 4:23, GNT).

The information and inspiration you expose your mind to determine the fruit your mind will produce. Positive thinking aligns your mind with faith and expectancy.

After praying in faith, never permit a mental picture of failure to linger in your mind. If doubt arises, rebuke it and refocus on God's promises. Remove every image, suggestion, vision, dream, impression, or thought that contradicts your faith. Your thoughts must affirm that you have already received what you asked for.

3. The fruit of the mouth: words.

"A man's belly shall be satisfied with the fruit of his mouth: and with the increase of his lips shall he be filled. Death and life are in the power of the tongue: and they that love it shall eat the fruit thereof" (Proverbs 18: 20-21, KJV).

Your words shape your destiny. They can be productive or destructive. We exercise dominion for fruitfulness through the words we speak.

Your words impact three realms: They confront satanic opposition; they activate angelic intervention; and they move heaven to act on your behalf.

When Daniel prayed, the angel told him, *"because of your words"* (Daniel 10:12)—his words triggered angelic response.

Even in difficulties, speak and declare that God is at work in your life. Your words are spiritual weapons. What you store in your heart determines the fruit of your mouth.

"Let the weak say I am strong" (Joel 3:10).

4. The fruit of the hands: work.

Some people labor but see no result because their hands are not blessed.

"Favour is deceitful, and beauty is vain: but a woman that feareth the Lord, she shall be praised. Give her of the fruit of her hands; and let her own works praise her in the gates. (Proverbs 31: 30-31, KJV).

When your hands are blessed, you will work creatively, diligently, and productively.

"Say ye to the righteous, that it shall be well with him: for they shall eat the fruit of their doings" (Isaiah 3:10, KJV).

Your hard work, enterprise and industry produce the fruit of your hands

5. Fruit of the Spirit: character.

"But the fruit of the Spirit is love, joy, peace, longsuffering, kindness, goodness, faithfulness, gentleness, self-control. Against such there is no law" (Galatians 5:22-24).

God's work in your heart through His Spirit and grace must produce visible results. It should be evident in your character that you are a child of God.

Just as a tree is known by its fruit, your life should be a testimony of the Holy Spirit's active presence within you. The fruit of the Spirit is not a mere list of virtues—it is the tangible evidence of a transformed heart. When the Spirit works effectively in you, these nine attributes—love, joy, peace, patience, kindness, goodness, faithfulness, gentleness, and self-control—become your natural disposition, shaping how you think, speak, and act.

A life governed by the Spirit reflects Christ, drawing others to God. Your light will shine so brightly that people will see your good works—your transformed character—and glorify your Father in heaven. Let your life be a living testimony of God's work in you!

Essentially, to be truly fruitful, every part of your being must produce:

- Your womb (and loins) – biological fruitfulness
- Your mind – creative and strategic thinking
- Your mouth – words that shape reality
- Your hands – diligent work
- Your spirit – godly character

ACTIVATING THE COVENANT OF FRUITFULNESS

Fruitfulness is not passive; it is activated!

"…The kingdom of heaven suffers violence, and the violent take it by force" (Matthew 11:12).

So, how do you activate this covenant of fruitfulness?

1. Engage in soul winning.

God is a rewarder, not a robber (Hebrews 11:6). If you serve Him, He will reward you. The Shunamite woman was rewarded (2 Kings 4:8-37). Zechariah served God and John the Baptist was born. Abraham served and Isaac came.

147

2. Make a demand for fruitfulness.

"Ask, and it will be given to you; seek, and you will find; knock, and it will be opened to you. For everyone who asks receives, and he who seeks finds, and to him who knocks it will be opened" (Matthew 7:7-8).

"You have not because you ask not" (James 4:2).

"Now Isaac pleaded with the LORD for his wife, because she was barren; and the LORD granted his plea, and Rebekah his wife conceived" (Genesis 25:21).

"For this child I prayed, and the Lord granted my request" (1 Samuel 1:27). Be specific about what you want. What you don't want, you don't watch. What you don't confront has the right to remain.

3. Believe against all odds.

Natural, medical, spiritual or any other.

Faith is your access to a world of unlimited possibilities. *"If you can believe, all things are possible to him who believes"* (Mark 9:23).

4. Let your confidence in God be unshakeable.

"Against all hope, Abraham in hope believed and so became the father of many nations, just as it had been said to him, "So shall your offspring be." Without weakening in his faith, he faced the fact that his body was as good as dead —since he was about a hundred years old —and that Sarah's womb was also dead. Yet he did not waver through unbelief regarding the

promise of God, but was strengthened in his faith and gave glory to God, being fully persuaded that God had power to do what he had promised" (Romans 4:18-21, NIV).

5. Ignore negative reports.

Medical science is limited. Whatever you may hear, believe only what God has said concerning you in His word. *"Who has believed our report?*

And to whom has the arm of the LORD been revealed?" (Isaiah 53:1). Continually saturate your spirit with God's promises.

6. Remain at peace with God and with yourself.

God works in us when we are at rest. Your relaxation in God determines your acceleration. *"Do not be afraid. Stand still, and see the salvation of the LORD, which He will accomplish for you today. For the Egyptians whom you see today, you shall see again no more forever. The LORD will fight for you, and you shall hold your peace"* (Exodus 14:13-14).

7. No offense towards God and people.

Let go and let God. *"And herein do I exercise myself, to have always a conscience void of offence toward God, and toward men"* (Acts 24:16).

8. Rejoice always.

Merriment is medicinal. Joy is required to lay hold of our fruitfulness. *"Rejoice in the Lord always. Again I will say, rejoice!"* (Philippians 4:4).

> *"And she said, "Let your maidservant find favor in your sight." So the woman went her way and ate, and her face was no longer sad."* (1 Samuel 1:18).

Joy is a sweet-smelling savor. A joyful heart attracts divine intervention.

CHAPTER 12

THE PROMISE OF TERRITORIAL DOMINION

"After the death of Moses the servant of the LORD, it came to pass that the LORD spoke to Joshua the son of Nun, Moses assistant, saying, Moses My servant is dead. Now therefore, arise, go over this Jordan, you and all this people, to the land which I am giving to them. Every place that the sole of your foot will tread upon I have given you, as I said to Moses."

(Joshua 1:1-3)

With Moses gone, the mantle of leadership passed to Joshua. In verse 3, we see that God's promise of territorial dominion extends to us today.

Kingdom advancement is territorial. You must understand the power of territorial dominion. There is a particular understanding you must have to possess the land God has given to you. You remain a stranger in a territory until the land receives you.

Territorial dominion is taking charge of a particular territory. And before you can take charge of that territory, you must know that there is a principality in charge of it. This means that you cannot just wake up and say you want to take charge of a territory without having full knowledge and taking decisive action. It doesn't work that way. Before you dominate a territory, you must be spiritually licensed to do so. Divine authority is required.

> " Now the LORD spoke to Moses in the plains of Moab by the Jordan, across from Jericho, saying, "Speak to the children of Israel, and say to them: When you have crossed the Jordan into the land of Canaan, then you shall drive out all the inhabitants of the land from before you, destroy all their engraved stones, destroy all their molded images, and demolish all their high places; you shall dispossess the inhabitants of the land and dwell in it, for I have given you the land to possess" (Numbers 33:50-53).

There must be an instruction from God before you can successfully invade any section of the cosmos. A believer with an improper understanding of his or her entitlement cannot dominate a territory because territorial invasion is done by knowledge.

> "Behold, I give you the authority to trample on serpents and scorpions, and over all the power of the enemy, and nothing shall by any means hurt you" (Luke 10:19).

Since God has given us dominion, what should we do? We must walk in the light of understanding. We are not called to wish for dominion but to step into it. And we must do so with confidence. "Wherever you step into, you have dominion." Most importantly, we must exercise our divine authority. We don't need permission from the enemy—we already have authority over him!

WHERE IS YOUR LICENSE?

If you have not been licensed, then please don't try to dominate a territory. There is a difference between knowing you have dominion and invading that territory. Remember, in every territory, there is a ruling principality. They determine who and what goes in and out of a territory. They decide the activities that take place there.

Therefore, for you to invade a territory, knowledge is not enough. You must understand the systems that govern such territories in order to break into them. Remember, we are not asking for permission to enter—we have been given authority over them. We invade, and doing so requires a higher level of spiritual intelligence.

A territory can reject you if you fail to understand its governing systems. If I am to break out of a prison, I need to know the exit point. It would be in one of two places: either you face the main exit or you escape. However, the concept of territorial dominion is not about secrecy—it is intentional. Escaping is not territorial dominion. We move to the main exit, break every hold of principalities and powers, and displace them.

To take over a land in the Middle Ages and earlier, a king had to defeat another king and take over the land of the conquered. Similarly, you cannot take over a territory by attempting to make a physical impact first. You must first deal with the spiritual principality that governs that territory. Only after assuming the position of the new principality in the spiritual realm can you take over physically. Once you have become a spiritual authority in that territory, the cosmos will respond to your declarations concerning it.

> *"And raised us up together, and made us sit together in the heavenly places in Christ Jesus"* (Ephesians 2:6).

Ephesians clearly tells us that we are now seated above principalities and powers. So why do these territories remain under the control of these forces? The answer is simple: the children of God have refused to take up their leadership roles.

Ignorance is bad, but worse still is knowing your identity and failing to act on it. Believers have lost their authority because they have remained passive.

There are principles of territorial dominion. Luke 8:22-24 shows us that Jesus was a man who commanded territories—and we also understand that Jesus was a man of prayer. You cannot command influence in a territory if you are not a person of prayer.

THE POWER OF PRAYER

One of the principles for territorial dominion is the power of prayer. It takes warfare to deal with the principalities and powers in a territory. We take territories when we understand the warfare dimension of prayer. This warfare dimension occurs when we manipulate spiritual possibilities to align with God's agenda.

There are gates that are not meant to be opened—they must be broken! You must wage war in the place of prayer.

You should not be passive when it comes to Kingdom advancement. Soldiers, wake up! Enough is enough!

What do you think the Bible means when it says:

> *"...since the days of John the Baptist, the Kingdom of God suffers violence, and the violent take it by force"* (Matthew 11:12)?

It means that for the advancement of the Kingdom, violent men in the secret place must arise—watchmen who are relentless, ensuring that God's will emerges strongly and accurately.

It is heartbreaking to see believers rendered powerless by the forces governing their territories—unable to subdue what they have already been given dominion over. If the forces fighting against your destiny are not subdued, no territory will receive you.

We do not war against flesh and blood. Both spiritual and physical territories are contended for. You cannot invade without being a person of prayer—you will be rejected.

Prayer releases a dimension of power so strong that it can injure the forces acting as principalities in a territory. A man of dominion does not wait for battles to come to him—he takes the fight to the enemy.

Do you want advancement? As soldiers, we are to march to the gates of hell and break them down!

Are you a soldier? Are you the one who understands that the believer's authority means you have already been given dominion? It's not that God will give it—it's that He has already given it!

A JOSHUA GENERATION HAS BEEN BORN

Prophetically speaking, a Joshua generation has been born - one that will invade territories. Go and speak over that territory! Have you forgotten that your words are spirit and life (John 6:63)? We are born to dominate. God's original purpose for humanity was dominion. If we do not have it now, it means we have strayed from God's command—and we need to return to it.

Let the principalities know your spiritual identity. WHO ARE YOU?

"Jesus I know, and Paul I know; but who are you?" (Acts 19:15)

Have you made an impact in the realm of the spirit?

This is not about living a passive Christian life. We must be aggressive about Kingdom advancement in the secret place.

God has already set the fire. Altars are burning now. Get set on fire!

AUTHORIZED TO REIGN ON GOD'S BEHALF

"For He has not put the world to come, of which we speak, in subjection to angels. But one testified in a certain place, saying: "What is man that You are mindful of him, Or the son of man that You take care of him? You have made him a little lower than the angels; You have crowned him with glory and honor, And set him over the works of Your hands. You have put all things in subjection under his feet." For in that He put all in subjection under him, He left nothing that is not put under him. But now we do not yet see all things put under him" (Hebrews 2:5-8).

Man lost his dominion mandate due to Adam's disobedience. But by redemption, what Adam lost, Jesus Christ restored. What we lost in Adam has been regained—and in Christ, it is even better!

"Therefore, just as through one man sin entered the world, and death through sin, and thus death spread to all men, because all sinned… For as by one man's disobedience many were made sinners, so also by one Man's obedience many will be made righteous (Romans 5:12, 19).

The fall removed us from the throne but redemption brought us back into it. The first Adam caused us to lose dominion but the last Adam brought us back into dominion.

Redemption is the recovery of your dominion mandate—the right to rule, the right to be victorious, and the right to prosper. By redemption, we are the ambassadors of God's Kingdom on the earth.

"Now then, we are ambassadors for Christ, as though God were pleading through us: we implore you on Christ's behalf, be reconciled to God" (2 Corinthians 5:20).

We are not just citizens of God's Kingdom on the earth; we are His ambassadors. This means that even though we live on the earth, our true existence is not of this earth.

"They are not of the world, just as I am not of the world. Sanctify them by Your truth. Your word is truth. As You sent Me into the world, I also have sent them into the world" (John 17:16-18).

Though we are in the world, we are not of the world. We are seated far above all demonic forces (Ephesians 1:21).

The least born-again Christian is higher than the highest occult power. Redemption has marked us as peculiar citizens of the earth.

"And hath raised us up together, and made us sit together in heavenly places in Christ Jesus." —Ephesians 2:6

LEVELS OF DOMINION

As believers, we have been authorized to reign at three levels. We are to reign over Satan, systems and situations.

REIGNING OVER SATAN AND SPIRITS (THE ATMOSPHERE OF YOUR REGION)

By redemption, you have been authorized with power over the forces of darkness. You are empowered to triumph over the forces of evil, witchcraft, and opposition.

" Then He called His twelve disciples together and gave them power and authority over all demons, and to cure diseases" (Luke 9:1).

" Behold, I give you the authority to trample on serpents and scorpions, and over all the power of the enemy, and nothing shall by any means hurt you" (Luke 10:19).

REIGNING OVER SYSTEMS

You have been authorized to govern and rule over systems— economic, political, financial, artistic, media, educational, fashion, and more. These systems were instituted by God, though Satan attempts to manipulate them.

As kings and priests, our role is to subdue the earth for God, not for self-glory, but to bring the world under His dominion. As a Kingdom citizen, you are empowered to birth God's purpose on earth and enforce His will—over nations, your family, and your personal life. Dominion makes you a territorial commander, ensuring that what God has determined and declared is what manifests in the earth.

"After this manner therefore pray ye: Our Father which art in heaven, Hallowed be thy name. Thy kingdom come, Thy will be done in earth, as it is in heaven" (Matthew 6:9-10, KJV).

Understanding dominion enables you to maintain authority over your God-given domain and sphere of influence. You must consciously recognize that you are a watchman over your region. We are enforcers of God's will.

"I have set watchmen upon thy walls, O Jerusalem, which shall never hold their peace day nor night: ye that make mention of the Lord, keep not silence, And give him no rest, till he establish, and till he make Jerusalem a praise in the earth" (Isaiah 62:6-7, KJV).

Pray and decree the agenda of God over your city, neighborhood and workplace. By reason of dominion, only man can partner with God for His will and purpose to be done on the earth (I Timothy 2:1-3. Daniel 10:13).

REIGNING OVER SITUATIONS (IT'S UNDER MY FEET)

Understanding your dominion mandate will help you reject limitations you may have previously accepted. It equips you to subdue life's challenges rather than be subdued by them.

Everything has been placed under Jesus' feet – and since we are a part of the Body of Christ, all things are under our feet as well. It doesn't matter what type of problem comes against us—whether physical, emotional, financial, or familial—we have been given the authority to walk in victory over them.

"Which he wrought in Christ, when he raised him from the dead, and set him at his own right hand in the heavenly places, Far above all principality, and power, and might, and dominion, and every name that is named, not only in this world, but also in that which is to come: And hath put all things under his feet, and gave him to be the head over all things to the church, Which is his body, the fulness of him that filleth all in all" (Ephesians 1:20-23, KJV).

160

Your perception of challenges determines whether you emerge victorious or defeated. It is easy to become overwhelmed, but remember:

> *"For he hath put all things under his feet..."* 1 Corinthians 15:27-28

> *"And the God of peace shall bruise Satan under your feet shortly"* (Romans 16:20).

The word "bruise" (Greek: suntribo) means to break into pieces, crush, shatter, demolish, or trample. This signifies total conquest.

> *"And he said unto them, I beheld Satan as lightning fall from heaven. Behold, I give unto you power to tread on serpents and scorpions, and over all the power of the enemy: and nothing shall by any means hurt you"* (Luke 10:18-19, KJV)

> Psalms 91:13 further says, *"Thou shalt tread upon the lion and adder"* (KJV).

Lions and adders symbolize Satan and his demonic hosts— yet we are given authority to tread upon them. To tread on something means it is beneath you.

YOUR DOMINION IN CHRIST

1. Dominion Over Sicknesses And Diseases.

Jesus Christ has paid the price for our sickness and diseases (Matthew 8:17).

161

God's will for us as believers is to live in perfect health. Before the arrival of any sickness, Christ already paid the price.

2. Dominion Over Obstacles, Hinderances, And Temptations.

They are no match for you. Nothing will keep you from fulfilling destiny.

3. Dominion Over Failures And Missteps.

Failures and missteps in life can also sting. They can crush us and keep us from moving forward. But by dominion, we have authority to tread on the mistakes we've made. We can step over failures and rise up in victory through Christ.

> *"Rejoice not against me, O mine enemy: when I fall, I shall arise; when I sit in darkness, the Lord shall be a light unto me"* (Micah 7:8).

4. Dominion Over Poisonous Words And Lies From Men.

The Bible likens slander and false accusations to venom. *"The poison of asps is under their lips"* (Romans 3:13). When faced with false accusations, remember: **you have the power to rise above the lies.** Hurtful words do not define you—**God's Word does.**

HOW TO GROW IN DOMINION AND GLORY

1. Develop the "I am from above" mindset.

Your mindset determines your destiny. You are an ambassador

of God's kingdom on earth, backed by the resources of heaven. You are not affected by the economy of this land. "*For our citizenship is in heaven, from which we also eagerly wait for the Savior, the Lord Jesus Christ*" (Philippians 3:20).

All the embassies and the ambassadors of nations of the earth are sustained by the resources of their country. They earn what they earn from their country. By redemption, you are a peculiar citizen of the earth. You have been delivered from the kingdom of darkness and translated to that of God's dear Son (Colossians 1:13).You live in Goshen (Genesis 47:27).

Hebrews 12:2 says, "*Looking unto Jesus, the author and finisher of our faith …*" That means whatever cannot be seen in Christ should not be seen in you. As the Father had sent Him so has He sent you (John 17:18). Can you imagine Jesus in a car wreck or on a hospital bed? I could not imagine Jesus, saying to Peter, James and John, "Do you have any bread there so I won't die of hunger?"

As an ambassador of God's Kingdom on the earth, you have heavenly immunity. The ambassadorial mindset means divine exemption. "I am divinely exempted".

> "*He who comes from above is above all; he who is of the earth is earthly and speaks of the earth. He who comes from heaven is above all*" (John 3:31).

It was for this reason that God exempted Israel from all the plagues that came upon Egypt. Exodus 9:24-26, for example, says: "*So there was hail, and fire mingled with the hail, so very heavy that there was none like it in all the land of Egypt since it became a nation. And the hail struck throughout the whole land of Egypt, all that was in the field, both man and beast; and the hail struck every herb of the field and broke every tree of the field. Only in the land of Goshen, where the children of Israel were, there was no hail."*

Hail brings devastation and destruction but it didn't get to where God's covenant people were. And God has assured us in Malachi 3:6, *"For I am the LORD, I do not change."* He remains ever committed to do the same for every believer today.

Again, Exodus 10:21-23 says, *"Then the LORD said to Moses, "Stretch out your hand toward heaven, that there may be darkness over the land of Egypt, darkness which may even be felt." So Moses stretched out his hand toward heaven, and there was thick darkness in all the land of Egypt three days. They did not see one another; nor did anyone rise from his place for three days. But all the children of Israel had light in their dwellings."*

When the world lacks knowledge and understanding of what to do, there will always be creativity and innovations in the Church that will lead the world.

2. Cultivate the "I am from above" lifestyle.

This must go together with the "I am from above" mentality. You must consciously and consistently choose to live a life that honors God—a life of faith and righteousness.

"For behold, the day is coming, burning like an oven, and all the proud, yes, all who do wickedly will be stubble. And the day which is coming shall burn them up," says the Lord of hosts, "That

164

will leave them neither root nor branch. But to you who fear My name, the Sun of Righteousness shall arise with healing in His wings; and you shall go out and grow fat like stall-fed calves" (Malachi 4:1-2)

3. Adopt the "I am from above" language.

Your words shape your reality. Speak words of faith and authority.

"You will also declare a thing, and it will be established for you; so light will shine on your ways. When they cast you down, and you say, 'Exaltation will come!' then He will save the humble person" (Job 22:28-29).

Have faith in the blood covenant of Jesus Christ. Always remain under its covering. The blood covenant is the highest and purest form of divine agreement. Every promise in God's Word is rooted in the power of this covenant.

4. Develop your divinity.

A lion cub can be killed by a confident goat if it fails to recognize its identity.

Your spiritual authority is largely determined by what you feed on. Do not be spiritually malnourished.

"Man shall not live by bread alone, but by every word that proceeds from the mouth of God" (Matthew 4:4)

"So now, brethren, I commend you to God and to the word of His grace, which is able to build you up and give you an inheritance

among all those who are sanctified" (Acts 20:32)

The difference between the first Adam and the last Adam (Jesus Christ) was spiritual growth. Feed your spirit with revelation, not just information.

> *"The entrance of Your words gives light; it gives understanding to the simple."* (Psalm 119:130).

When you meditate on and receive divine truth, it illuminates your spirit, activates the God-life within you, and disarms the forces of darkness.

> *"This is the message which we have heard from Him and declare to you, that God is light and in Him is no darkness at all"* (1 John 1:5).

You have been prayed for enough; it is time to rise up and take dominion. You are not a liability but an asset to the Kingdom. There is no situation confronting you that lacks a solution. Move beyond surface-level prayer. At every new level, there is an adversary, and you can only prevail through intensified prayer.

Establish a consistent prayer lifestyle—not just a crisis-driven prayer habit.

How do you develop your divinity?

- **Change your thinking** – Your thoughts shape your reality. Renovate your mind with the truth of God's Word.

- **Align your core beliefs** – Your beliefs influence your decisions, and your decisions determine your destiny.

5. Engage the person and power of the Holy Spirit.

The transactions of God's Kingdom are spiritual; they require the involvement of the Holy Spirit. It takes the Spirit to birth spiritual realities.

The Holy Spirit is the Carrier, Communicator, Transmitter, and Administrator of God's Kingdom on earth. He is the power from on high, and whatever is from above is above all.

When the Holy Spirit is at work in your life, nothing is permitted to resist your progress, success, accomplishments, or breakthroughs. The early apostles were ordinary men, but when they were filled with the Holy Spirit, they became extraordinary.

Undeniable exploits in the Kingdom are effortless when we are continually filled with and yielded to the Holy Spirit. Let Him reveal the deep things of God to you and grant you supernatural insights that will elevate you above your peers.

> *"But we all, with unveiled face, beholding as in a mirror the glory of the Lord, are being transformed into the same image from glory to glory, just as by the Spirit of the Lord"* (2 Corinthians 3:18).

The greatest power Jesus has given us is the power to become children of God.

"He came to His own, and His own did not receive Him. But as many as received Him, to them He gave the right to become children of God, to those who believe in His name: who were born, not of blood, nor of the will of the flesh, nor of the will of man, but of God" (John 1:11-13)

Have you received this power to become a child of God? You can make that decision today by surrendering your life to Jesus Christ. Accept Him as your Lord and Savior, and your name will be written in the Book of Life. Heaven will rejoice at your new birth! This is the greatest decision you can ever make. Joy will flood your heart on earth and for eternity.

6. Walk in boldness.

Be bold to do what God has commanded you, regardless of the prevailing circumstances.

"The wicked flee when no one pursues, but the righteous are bold as a lion" (Proverbs 28:1).

Self-confidence relies on what you can do in your own strength. Boldness, however, is confidence in what God can do through you.

Supernatural courage is the result of fellowship with Jesus.

"Now when they saw the boldness of Peter and John, and perceived that they were uneducated and untrained men, they marveled. And they realized that they had been with Jesus" (Acts 4:13).

God may command you to do things that do not align with

human wisdom, but you must be bold enough to step out in faith. When Jesus told Peter to walk on water, Peter obeyed and experienced the supernatural.

There are territories, industries, and nations waiting for you to take dominion. You must hear from God and move forward in boldness.

Fear is not from God; it is a tool of the enemy.

> *"For God has not given us a spirit of fear, but of power and of love and of a sound mind"* (2 Timothy 1:7).

You are authorized to reign. You have been given dominion. Live with the mindset, language, and power of one who is from above. Align your thinking, develop your divine nature, engage the Holy Spirit, and walk boldly in your God-given authority.

May you arise and take your place as a Kingdom ambassador, enforcing God's will on earth as it is in heaven. Amen!

CHAPTER 13

THE PROMISE OF PEACE

"Peace I leave with you. My peace I give to you; not
as the world gives do I give to you. Let not your heart
be troubled, neither let it be afraid."

(John 14:27)

In life, you are either full of fear or full of peace. Peace is a
precious gift that everyone longs for. We all desire peace of
mind. We seek peace in our relationships, in our workplaces, in
our families, and within our own hearts. But true peace is not
merely the absence of trouble—it is the presence of God in
the midst of it.

*"But now the LORD my God has given me rest on every side;
there is neither adversary nor evil occurrence"* (1 Kings 5:4).

When our peace is disturbed, we often feel unbalanced and
unsettled. You may have experienced situations that almost
robbed you of your peace, or perhaps you are in one right

now. Are you troubled by uncertainties about the future? Do you feel anxious, fearful, or overwhelmed? Are you panicking because of an unexpected crisis?

Just as Jesus commanded the storm to be still, I decree peace over your life today.

> *"Then He arose and rebuked the wind, and said to the sea, 'Peace, be still!' And the wind ceased and there was a great calm"* (Mark 4:39).

I pray that the peace of God, which surpasses all understanding, will guard your heart and mind (Philippians 4:7). This is not a temporary or circumstantial peace but a supernatural peace—a peace that allows you to remain at rest despite life's storms, a peace that frees you to enjoy life, family, and friends. This peace is not dependent on external situations; it comes only from God.

GOD'S REASSURING PEACE

God's peace is not based on human logic. It is a solid confidence in God that enables you to declare:

> *"The LORD is my helper; I will not fear. What can man do to me?"* (Hebrews 13:6).

The peace from above is a resolute faith in God's sovereignty—a trust that no matter what you face, God is faithful. It is a faith that looks beyond present challenges and sees the hand of God working all things together for good.

"God is our refuge and strength, a very present help in trouble. Therefore we will not fear, even though the earth be removed, and though the mountains be carried into the midst of the sea; though its waters roar and be troubled, though the mountains shake with its swelling. Selah. There is a river whose streams shall make glad the city of God, the holy place of the tabernacle of the Most High. God is in the midst of her, she shall not be moved; God shall help her, just at the break of dawn" (Psalm 46:1-5).

This is the peace that sustains you in the cancer ward, the bankruptcy court, or even in the valley of loss and grief. The world's peace is fragile, dependent on favorable circumstances. When things are going well, people feel at peace. But when trouble comes, that peace vanishes. Jesus made a clear distinction between His peace and the world's fleeting peace:

"Peace I leave with you, My peace I give to you; not as the world gives do I give to you. Let not your heart be troubled, neither let it be afraid."

The peace that comes from a right relationship with God is unshakable because it is rooted in His eternal promises.

HOW TO EXPERIENCE GOD'S PEACE

God does not want you to live in worry or anxiety. He calls you to a life of peace by trusting Him in every situation.

"Be anxious for nothing, but in everything by prayer and supplication, with thanksgiving, let your requests be made known to God; and the peace of God, which surpasses all understanding, will guard your hearts and minds through Christ Jesus. Finally,

brethren, whatever things are true, whatever things are noble, whatever things are just, whatever things are pure, whatever things are lovely, whatever things are of good report, if there is any virtue and if there is anything praiseworthy—meditate on these things. The things which you learned and received and heard and saw in me, these do, and the God of peace will be with you" (Philippians 4:6-9)

The Greek word for "anxious" in this passage means **to be troubled with cares.** When you worry, you shift your focus away from God's goodness and promises. Worry fills your mind with negative thoughts that do not align with the standard set in Philippians 4:8. Instead of dwelling on fear, focus on faith.

1. Turn your cares into prayers.

Instead of worrying, bring your concerns before God in prayer.

"Casting all your care upon Him, for He cares for you" (1 Peter 5:7).

Prayer shifts your burdens from your shoulders to God's. When you lay everything before Him in faith, His peace will guard your heart and mind.

2. Cultivate a heart of thanksgiving.

Thanksgiving is a powerful expression of faith. Abraham gave glory to God **before** he saw the fulfillment of God's promise.

"He did not waver at the promise of God through unbelief, but was strengthened in faith, giving glory to God, and being fully convinced that what He had promised He was also able to perform" (Romans 4:20-21)

Learn to thank God, not just for what He has done, but for what He has promised to do. His Word is as certain as its fulfillment.

3. Focus on God's promises.

Train your mind to dwell on God's Word rather than on negative circumstances.

"You will keep him in perfect peace, whose mind is stayed on You, because he trusts in You" (Isaiah 26:3).

Peace is not found in the absence of problems but in the presence of God. The more you meditate on His truth, the more your heart will be anchored in peace.

4. Put God's Word into practice.

It is not enough to hear or read about peace—you must walk in it.

"Now may the Lord of peace Himself give you peace always in every way. The Lord be with you all" (2 Thessalonians 3:16).

God's peace is not just an abstract concept; it is a daily reality for those who put His Word into practice.

MAKING PEACE WITH GOD

The best place to start your journey to true peace is by making peace with God.

> *"Therefore, having been justified by faith, we have peace with God through our Lord Jesus Christ"* (Romans 5:1).

You can only experience the peace of God when you have peace with God. If you have never surrendered your life to Jesus, now is the time.

Say this prayer:

> *"Lord Jesus, I acknowledge that I need Your peace. I surrender my life to You and accept You as my Lord and Savior. Forgive me of my sins, and fill my heart with Your peace. I choose to trust You with my life. Thank You for loving me and giving me eternal life. In Jesus' name, Amen."*

If you prayed this prayer, welcome to the family of God! Heaven rejoices over your decision, and His peace will now reign in your heart.

May the Lord bless you and fill your life with His perfect peace—peace that overcomes, peace that endures, and peace that will never fail. Amen!

CHAPTER 14

THE PROMISE OF GOOD HEALTH

"Beloved, I wish above all things that thou mayest prosper and be in health, even as thy soul prospereth."

(3 John 1:2, KJV)

God prioritizes your well-being. After your salvation, the next greatest desire of God for you is the prosperity of your health. He wants us to live free of sickness and disease because He understands their devastating effects on our lives. Divine health is not just a possibility—it is God's will for His children. He accomplishes our healing through several channels.

To fully grasp the promise of divine health, we must first understand the origin and composition of man.

THE COMPOSITION OF MAN

In Genesis 1:27 and Genesis 2:7, we see that man was both created and formed by God:

- **Genesis 1:27** – *"So God created man in His own image; in the image of God He created him; male and female He created them."*

- **Genesis 2:7** – *"And the LORD God formed man of the dust of the ground, and breathed into his nostrils the breath of life; and man became a living being."*

The Hebrew word for "created" (*bara*) means to **form something out of nothing**, while "formed" (*asah*) means to **fashion something out of pre-existing material**. God created our spirit, formed our body, and breathed into us, making us living beings. This means that both our spiritual and physical health matter to God.

THE TRUE SOURCE OF HEALTH

From the beginning, the sustenance of our health was never meant to depend on medicine or human remedies alone but on **God's word.**

> *"…Man shall not live by bread alone, but by every word that proceeds from the mouth of God"* (Matthew 4:4).

God's Word is a life-giving force, capable of healing and sustaining the body:

> *"My son, give attention to my words; incline your ear to my sayings. Do not let them depart from your eyes; keep them in the midst of your heart; for they are life to those who find them, and health to all their flesh"* (Proverbs 4:20-22).

When Jesus walked the earth, He healed the sick not just

through physical touch but also by His word:

"When evening had come, they brought to Him many who were demon-possessed. And He cast out the spirits with a word, and healed all who were sick" (Matthew 8:16).

God's word is the container of healing power, and His commands are not just instructions but enablements that bring healing.

THE DIVINE EXCHANGE AT THE CROSS

Jesus defeated Satan, sin, and sickness through His work on the cross so that we could live the resurrected life. His victory is total and complete:

"But thanks be to God, who gives us the victory through our Lord Jesus Christ" (1 Corinthians 15:57).

The cross is the greatest **exchange** in history, where Jesus took upon Himself our burdens and gave us His blessings. This exchange is described in *Isaiah 53:3-5*:

"He is despised and rejected by men, a Man of sorrows and acquainted with grief... Surely He has borne our griefs and carried our sorrows; yet we esteemed Him stricken, smitten by God, and afflicted. But He was wounded for our transgressions, He was bruised for our iniquities; the chastisement for our peace was upon Him, and by His stripes we are healed."

THE SEVEN-FOLD EXCHANGE
ON THE CROSS

- **Death for Life** – Jesus took our death so we could have eternal life (*Hebrews 2:14-15, Revelation 1:18*).

- **Curse for Blessing** – He became a curse so that we might receive Abraham's blessing (*Galatians 3:13-14*).

- **Sickness for Health** – He bore our sickness so we could walk in divine health (*Matthew 8:17*).

- **Rejection for Acceptance** – God turned His back on Jesus so we would never be forsaken (*Ephesians 1:6*).

- **Poverty for Prosperity** – He became poor so we could have all we need (*2 Corinthians 8:9*).

- **Defeat for Victory** – Through Christ, we overcome all challenges (*Romans 8:37*).

- **Bondage for Freedom** – Jesus set us free from sin and oppression (*John 8:36*).

As believers, it is our **birthright** to walk in these blessings.

HEALING IS PART OF REDEMPTION

Divine healing is not just an Old Testament concept. It is part of our New Covenant inheritance. In Isaiah 53:4-5, the words "griefs" and "sorrows" translate to sickness (choli) and pain (makob), emphasizing that Jesus bore not only our sins but also our infirmities.

This was confirmed in the ministry of Jesus:

180

"That it might be fulfilled which was spoken by Isaiah the prophet, saying: 'He Himself took our infirmities and bore our sicknesses'" (Matthew 8:17).

Jesus made healing a **sign** of those who believe:

"And these signs will follow those who believe: In My name they will cast out demons... they will lay hands on the sick, and they will recover" (Mark 16:17-18).

Healing did not end with Jesus' ministry—it continues through His disciples.

UNDERSTANDING THE CAUSES OF SICKNESS

Not all sicknesses are the same. Here are five possible causes of sickness:

1. Poor Diet And Lifestyle.

- Many diseases today stem from unhealthy food choices.
- Genesis 1:29 shows that God originally designed natural foods to sustain us.

2. Genetics And Generational Curses.

- Some diseases are passed down in families, but the blood of Jesus breaks generational curses.
- Deuteronomy 5:9-10 reminds us that blessings replace curses in Christ.

3. Demonic Strongholds Or Spirit Of Infirmity.

- Some illnesses are caused by spiritual oppression, as seen in Luke 13:10-16.

- Jesus identified and cast out the spirit of infirmity, bringing healing.

4. Sin And Lack Of Spiritual Covering.

- Unrepented sin can open doors to affliction (*John 5:14*).

- Rebellion against God's authority can also lead to vulnerability (James 4:7).

5. Natural Birth Defects.

- Some sicknesses exist from birth, but God can still heal and restore (John 9:1-3).

HOW GOD HEALS

God uses various methods to bring healing. Jesus spoke, laid hands, spat, and even used mud. Healing is often a process, while miracles are instantaneous.

1. **Through proper diet, exercise, and lifestyle**. Taking care of your body is a way to honor the temple God has entrusted to you. Balanced nutrition, regular physical activity, and healthy habits contribute to physical well-being, creating the conditions for natural healing and sustained health. "*Therefore, whether you eat or drink, or whatever you do, do all to the glory of God*" (1 Corinthians 10:31).

2. **Through walking in forgiveness and grace**. Emotional and spiritual health often influences physical health.

Choosing forgiveness and extending grace can ease the burden of resentment and stress, promoting inner peace. This fosters holistic healing and aligns you with God's desire for restoration and harmony. "Let all bitterness, wrath, anger, clamor, and evil speaking be put away from you, with all malice" (Ephesians 4:31).

3. **Through spiritual covering and connection to the Body of Christ.** *"Is anyone among you sick? Let him call for the elders of the church, and let them pray over him, anointing him with oil in the name of the Lord. And the prayer of faith will save the sick, and the Lord will raise him up. And if he has committed sins, he will be forgiven. Confess your trespasses to one another, and pray for one another, that you may be healed. The effective, fervent prayer of a righteous man avails much"* (James 5:14-16).

4. **Through doctors and medicine.** *"When Jesus heard it, He said to them, 'Those who are well have no need of a physician, but those who are sick…"* (Mark 2:17). However, while medical knowledge is highly beneficial, it has its limitations. Healing ultimately comes from God.

5. **Through faith in the name of Jesus.** *God has exalted the name of Jesus above all names, including that of any sickness* (Philippians 2:9). Most sicknesses are direct oppressions of the devil, and the name of Jesus is the master key to destroying his works.

"Most assuredly, I say to you, he who believes in Me, the works that I do he will do also; and greater works than these he will do, because I go to My Father. And whatever you ask in My name, that I will do, that the Father may be glorified in the Son. If you

183

ask anything in My name, I will do it" (John 14:12-14).

"And these signs will follow those who believe: In My name they will cast out demons; they will speak with new tongues; they will take up serpents; and if they drink anything deadly, it will by no means hurt them; they will lay hands on the sick, and they will recover" (Mark 16:17-18).

"And His name, through faith in His name, has made this man strong, whom you see and know. Yes, the faith which comes through Him has given him this perfect soundness in the presence of you all" (Acts 3:16).

6. **Through prayer, meditation on the Word, and faith-filled confession.** God's Word is the vehicle of healing grace. *"He sent His word and healed them, and delivered them from their destructions."* — Psalm 107:20)

   "When evening had come, they brought to Him many who were demon-possessed. And He cast out the spirits with a word, and healed all who were sick" (Matthew 8:16).

   "My son, give attention to my words; incline your ear to my sayings. Do not let them depart from your eyes; keep them in the midst of your heart; for they are life to those who find them, and health to all their flesh." (Proverbs 4:20-22).

Your healing is not determined by medical reports or human experiences, but by the Word of God.

7. **Through faith in the blood of Jesus.** Your healing is not in medicine or drugs but in redemption. Jesus already paid the price.

> *"Knowing that you were not redeemed with corruptible things, like silver or gold, from your aimless conduct received by tradition from your fathers, but with the precious blood of Christ, as of a lamb without blemish and without spot"* (1 Peter 1:18-19).

> *"That it might be fulfilled which was spoken by Isaiah the prophet, saying: 'He Himself took our infirmities and bore our sicknesses'"* (Matthew 8:17).

> *"Surely He has borne our griefs [Hebrew: choli—sickness] and carried our sorrows [Hebrew: makob—pain]; yet we esteemed Him stricken, smitten by God, and afflicted. But He was wounded for our transgressions, He was bruised for our iniquities; the chastisement for our peace was upon Him, and by His stripes we are healed"* (Isaiah 53:4-5). Medical conditions are categorized into 39 major disease groups—Jesus bore 40 stripes, ensuring healing for every category of disease, including any new ones that may arise.

8. **Through faith in the healing anointing.** Sickness is a yoke, and the anointing breaks every yoke. *"It shall come to pass in that day that his burden will be taken away from your shoulder, and his yoke from your neck, and the yoke will be destroyed because of the anointing..."* (Isaiah 10:27).

> *"How God anointed Jesus of Nazareth with the Holy Spirit and with power, who went about doing good and healing all who were oppressed by the devil, for God was with Him"* (Acts 10:38).

9. Through taking authority over the devil. Every time Jesus sent His disciples, He gave them power over unclean spirits and sickness. *"Behold, I give you the authority to trample on serpents and scorpions, and over all the power of the enemy, and nothing shall by any means hurt you"* (Luke 10:19).

    "Then He called His twelve disciples together and gave them power and authority over all demons, and to cure diseases. He sent them to preach the kingdom of God and to heal the sick" (Luke 9:1-2).

10. Through the spiritual gift of healing. Some believers are specially gifted with the ability to minister healing through the power of the Holy Spirit. *"There are diversities of gifts, but the same Spirit. There are differences of ministries, but the same Lord. And there are diversities of activities, but it is the same God who works all in all. But the manifestation of the Spirit is given to each one for the profit of all: for to one is given the word of wisdom through the Spirit, to another the word of knowledge through the same Spirit, to another faith by the same Spirit, to another gifts of healings by the same Spirit..."* (1 Corinthians 12:4-9).

RECEIVING HEALING BY FAITH

Whatever grace makes available is only obtainable by faith. *"Through whom also we have access by faith into this grace in which we stand, and rejoice in hope of the glory of God"* (Romans 5:2).

Faith activates healing. The duration of an illness does not determine the time it takes for healing.

- The lame man in Acts 3:2 had been crippled for over 40 years, yet he was healed instantly.

186

- The man at the Pool of Bethesda in John 5:5 suffered for 38 years but was healed in seconds.

- The woman with the issue of blood in Mark 5:25 suffered for 12 years but received healing instantly.

- The woman in Luke 13:11 had a spirit of infirmity for 18 years but was immediately healed.

FAITH IN ACTION

What To Do:

- Step out in faith. If you do what you can, God will do what you cannot.

- Move in faith—do what you couldn't do before.

- Stand firm in faith and avoid disobedience.

- Renew your mind with God's Word. *"And do not be conformed to this world, but be transformed by the renewing of your mind, that you may prove what is that good and acceptable and perfect will of God"* (Romans 12:2).

- Meditate on God's promises regarding health. *"For they are life to those who find them, and health to all their flesh"* (Proverbs 4:22).

Your healing is already secured by Christ's finished work. Believe, receive, and walk in divine health!